BARRON'S DOG BIBLES

Bulldogs

Phil Maggitti

BARRON'S

About the Author

Phil Maggitti is a freelance writer, editor, and occasional website designer living in southeastern Pennsylvania with his wife, three dogs, and four cats. He has written eight books and more than 800 articles since leaving his day job to write full time in 1982. Most of his work has explored the points at which the lives of humans and animals intersect.

Mr. Maggitti has written seven books for Barron's, including *Pugs: A Complete Pet Owner's Manual*, which was honored by the Dog Writer's Association as the best single-breed booklet in 1994. He also has received five awards from the American Horse Council for his equine writing.

All information and advice contained in this book has been reviewed by a veterinarian.

A Word About Pronouns

Many dog lovers feel that the pronoun "it" is not appropriate when referring to a pet that can be such a wonderful part of our lives. For this reason the Bulldog in this book is referred to as "he" unless the topic specifically relates to female dogs. This by no means implies any preference, nor should it be taken as an indication that either sex is particularly problematic.

Cover Credits
Front cover: Shutterstock; back cover: Tara Darling.

Photo Credits
Kent Dannen: page 114; Tara Darling: pages 2, 186; Cheryl A. Ertelt: page 102; Isabelle Francais: pages 34, 39, 156; Daniel Johnson: pages iii, vi, 6, 12, 16, 20, 21, 28, 31, 33, 36, 40, 44, 47, 48, 53, 58, 85, 87, 89, 91, 94, 99, 106, 109, 110, 119, 130 (top and bottom), 131 (top and bottom), 132 (top and bottom), 133 (top and bottom), 134 (top and bottom), 135 (top and bottom), 136, 139, 141, 142, 143, 150, 153, 154, 158, 161, 164, 167, 168, 175, 176; Paulette Johnson: pages i, 8, 18, 24, 43, 50, 54, 57, 62, 63, 67, 69, 71, 73, 77, 78, 93, 101, 127, 145, 147, 148, 152, 162, 173, 182; Connie Summers/Paulette Johnson: pages 5, 11, 67, 81.

All inquiries should be addressed to:
Barron's Educational Series, Inc.
250 Wireless Boulevard
Hauppauge, New York 11788
www.barronseduc.com

ISBN-10: 0-7641-6255-1 (Book)
ISBN-13: 978-0-7641-6255-8 (Book)
ISBN-10: 0-7641-8678-7 (DVD)
ISBN-13: 978-0-7641-8678-3 (DVD)
ISBN-10: 0-7641-9653-7 (Package)
ISBN-13: 978-0-7641-9653-9 (Package)

Library of Congress Catalog Card No: 2009007699

Library of Congress Cataloging-in-Publication Data
Maggitti, Phil.
  Bulldogs / Phil Maggitti.
    p. cm.— (Barron's breed bibles)
  Includes index.
  ISBN-13: 978-0-7641-6255-8 (bk)
  ISBN-10: 0-7641-6255-1 (bk)
  ISBN-13: 978-0-7641-8678-3 (DVD)
  ISBN-10: 0-7641-8678-7 (DVD)
  [etc.]
1. Bulldog. I. Title.

  SF429.B85M238 2009
  636.72—dc22
                                        2009007699

Printed in China

9 8 7 6 5 4

CONTENTS

CONTENTS

PREFACE

Given their long and demanding history of service to humankind, Bulldogs cannot be blamed for resting on their laurels and their favorite chair in the den. For three millennia—from the middle of the second century B.C.E. in the northwest corner of Greece to the middle of the nineteenth century in England—Bulldogs and their ancestors have paid their dues. They have guarded our houses and our possessions; they have followed us into battle; they have risked life and limb for our amusement; and they have given us a measure of loyalty and devotion scarcely seen in our fellow humans. Bulldogs have earned their rest. Long may they enjoy it.

Bulldogs became ladies and gentlemen of leisure abruptly in 1835, the point at which the British people finally had sent enough persons of goodwill to Parliament to secure the passage of the Animal Cruelty Act, which outlawed the "sport" of bullbaiting. In this unholy ritual a bull was tethered in the center of a ring, and then a Bulldog was sent into the ring to pin the bull by grabbing its muzzle and holding on until the bull was immobile. The bull, of course, tried to prevent this from happening by using its horns to rip the Bulldog open or toss him over the heads of the spectators. What irony—the same country that nurtured Shakespeare also nurtured bullbaiting.

The easygoing Bulldogs we see taking a walk with their owners today, if the weather is not too warm or humid, bear little resemblance to the dogs who participated in bullbaiting, and no resemblance to their statuesque Greek ancestors, the Molossian dogs. During the centuries since the Molossians were carried to the major ports of the world by Phoenician traders, the Bulldog's ancestors eventually were bred lower and lower, wider and wider—first in response to function, then in response to the dictates of fashion after bullbaiting had been outlawed.

Because fashion is often heedless of function, not to mention practicality, the Bulldog that was designed according to fashion's dictates cannot breed or deliver puppies without human assistance. That fashionable dog has a respiratory system compromised severely for the sake of a pretty face. He is, therefore, subject to breathing difficulties in hot or humid weather. He is plagued also by various joint, eye, and skin problems.

One aspect of the Bulldog that has not been "improved" is the breed's matchless personality, praised by Lord Byron (1788–1824) for embodying "Beauty without Vanity, Strength without Insolence, Courage without Ferocity, and all the Virtues of man without his Vices."

Any Bulldog owner will agree that the world would be a better place if people behaved more like Bulldogs—who are civil where we are often crabby, who are tenacious where we are likely to grow timid, and who are not cynical enough to believe that honesty is a policy, not a virtue. Besides, who could resist a dog that is known to use a bowling ball for a toy?

Chapter One

All About Bulldogs

Whenever the lives of humans and animals intersect, the fates of both are altered. Few dog breeds maximize the potential for that alteration as vividly as the Bulldog. Originally constructed for the violent and bloody work of bullbaiting—in which he was expected to immobilize a bull by chomping down on its nose and hanging on come hell or high water—the Bulldog was, upon threat of extinction, reconfigured into the happy-go-lucky sidekick that we know today.

During the course of that makeover, the Bulldog underwent physical and temperamental changes. The latter were primarily for the good, and the modern-day Bulldog is justly celebrated for his easygoing, fun-loving nature and his devotion to his people.

On the way to becoming a kinder, jollier sort, however—a transformation grounded in the virtues exhibited by his bullbaiting ancestors—the Bulldog was transformed physically into a near caricature of his former self. As early as 1927, Edward Ash wrote in *Dogs: Their History and Development*: "When bull-baiting ended, the dog was bred for [the] 'fancy,' and characteristics desired at earlier times for fighting and baiting purposes were exaggerated so that the unfortunate dog became unhappily abnormal. In this transition stage, huge, broad, ungainly heads were obtained, legs widely bowed were developed, and frequently the dog was a cripple."

In addition, the Bulldog's wrinkles, intended to channel the bull's blood away from the Bulldog's eyes, were greatly overemphasized. The layback of the face, which allowed Bulldogs to breathe while they hung on to a bull's nose, was also exaggerated; and the loose skin on the body, designed to protect the dog's internal organs during combat, grew even more loose and, therefore, more prone to infection.

The conditions described by Mr. Ash continue to shadow the Bulldog on both sides of the Atlantic today. The British, understandably, are more likely to take those conditions personally.

"The Bulldog of the 1800s was a potent symbol for our former imperial might," wrote Marcus Scriven in London's *Daily Mail*. "It was a brave fighter, with a longer muzzle than today's breed and possessed of a muscular agility second to none.

"Now, though, in what seems an inescapably apt metaphor for our decline, the British Bulldog is in dire trouble, its physique so damaged and distorted by inappropriate breeding that it has been reduced to a wheezing, loose-skinned parody of what it is meant to be . . . Today's dog suffers eye

problems, congenital heart conditions, dental and skin disorders, and verte-
brae deformities. Its shorter muzzle has led to breathing difficulties, and the
large head means pups have to be born by Caesarian section."

In spite of this list of complaints—which affect many Bulldogs some of
the time and some Bulldogs much of the time—the Bulldog is as popular
today as he has been at almost any time in his history. In 2008 he claimed a
place among the American Kennel Club's 10 most popular breeds, the first
time he had joined that club since 1935.

Such popularity cannot be credited solely to the Bulldog's good looks, his
profound snoring, or his legendary flatulence. Endearing as those qualities
may be, it is the Bully's personality that carries the day. Bulldog owners,
basking in their dogs' love, attention, and sound effects, know that if people
were more like Bulldogs, the world would be a better place. A rugged civil-
ity would reign in place of crabbiness; tenacity would dispatch timidity; loyalty would not be based solely on self-interest; people who snored would
have a ready cover; kids would have a hardy playmate; and honesty would
be a virtue, not a policy.

The Grecian Formula

The breed most often cited as the ancestor of today's Bulldog is the
Molossian, whose story begins near Epirus, in the northwest corner of
Greece, sometime between 1600 and 1100 B.C.E., but whose ultimate origin is
unknown. Molossians were conspicuous for their size, their courage as guard
dogs, and their ferocity in war. They became known as *Canis Molossi* because
they were kept by members of the Molossi tribe, who settled near Epirus.

FYI: Their Father Who Wert in Heaven

Molossian dogs were such imposing figures—in size and in action—that they acquired their own mythology. According to legend they were descended from a dog named Laeleps, who had been forged out of bronze by Hephaestus, the Greek god of fire.

Hephaestus did not create merely an impressive bit of sculpture. After he had fashioned Laeleps, he gave the dog a soul, then gifted him to Zeus, the supreme ruler of Mount Olympus, home of the gods. Not even supernatural dogs are safe from the whims of their masters, however, and after Laeleps had been passed along to several other owners, he was turned into stone—but not before he had sired a mighty race of dogs, the Molossians.

The Molossian was not destined to remain a local hero. Phoenician traders saw to that. The most skillful shipbuilders and navigators of their time, the Phoenicians occupied a ribbon of the Syrian coast—roughly 160 miles (260 km) long and 20 miles (32 km) wide—that now comprises Lebanon and parts of Syria and Israel.

Confined by their straitjacket turf, the Phoenicians turned to the sea to escape. They created a trading empire that spanned the known world, and they distributed all manner of goods throughout that world. Among those goods was the Molossian dog, who was carried to the British isles around 800 B.C.E. by Phoenician traders in search of tin.

Fun Facts

The Greeks were the first to write manuals about dogs. Aristotle, writing in 350 B.C.E. about the anatomy and physiology of the dog, listed the Molossian as one of the "most useful" known breeds.

From Battlefield to Bullring

The Molossian proved just as formidable in the British Isles as he had in Greece. When Roman invaders arrived in the British Isles in 50 C.E., they were met in battle by Molossian dogs who unseated many invaders by jumping up and putting a lip-lock on their horses' snouts. As a horse bucked and whirled and flailed about trying to dislodge the massive canine hanging from his nose, his rider was sent clattering to the ground.

The people of the British Isles thought this nose biting such a clever skill that they found a way to enjoy it in peace-time. That way was called bull-baiting, a "sport" in which a bull was set upon by dogs—usually in succession but sometimes in a pack. The bull was chained to an iron stake so that he could move in a circle covering roughly 30 feet (9 m) while a dog attempted to immobilize him by latching on to his nose, one of the more

3

FYI: The British Had a Word for It

The earliest reference to a Bulldog's ancestor in England appeared roughly 500 years ago in a poem titled "Cocke Lorelles Bote" (Cock Lorell's Boat). This poem, which spoofs lower-middle-class behavior, contains the following lines: "Than came one wt two bolddogges at his tayle/And that was a bocher without fayle."

The bolddogges that accompanied the bocher (butcher) also were known as *bon-dogges* or *bandogges* because they spent much of the day on a chain (banda). At night bandogges were released, the better to patrol their masters' properties. Shakespeare refers to this type of dog in *King Henry VI, Part II*, written between 1588 and 1590: "The time when screech owls and bandogges howl and spirits walk and ghosts break up their graves."

tender parts of his anatomy. A bull with a large dog hanging from its nose like a Christmas tree ornament is not going anywhere soon.

To be fair, the inhabitants of the British Isles did not invent this dodgy form of entertainment. Egyptians, Greeks, and Romans supported baiting, which sometimes involved bears, horses, and other animals in addition to bulls.

The bull might have been an unwilling participant in these contests, but he was not without resources. If a dog did not play his cards low to the ground, he could find himself disemboweled by one of the bull's horns or launched over the heads of the sportsmen who had gathered to wager and to cheer rabidly.

From the thirteenth through the mid-nineteenth century bullbaiting was the national pastime in England. Almost every town and village sported a bullring, where people of all social classes gathered to wager on bullbaiting.

The popularity of bullbaiting created a demand for dogs who were constructed to excel at this pursuit. Building on the courage, power, and ferocity of the Molossian, people began crossing their dogs with smaller breeds. One of those was possibly the Pug, who arrived in England in November 1688—and who, at the time, was taller than he is now.

Gradually the Molossian-type dog began to evolve toward the Bulldog breed as we know it today. His shoulders became set on the outside of his body, and his forelegs grew noticeably shorter than his hind legs, allowing him to crouch low enough to the ground to avoid the bull's horns when it charged. The bulk of the Bulldog's weight was shifted toward his head so that there was less chance of his back being snapped when a bull attempted to shake him off its nose.

Bullbaiting dogs underwent facial changes too. Their lower jaws gradually began to stick out farther than their upper jaws, allowing them to breathe even when they had a mouthful of bull nose. The increasingly deepened wrinkles on the dogs' faces channeled the bull's blood away from their eyes.

The End of an Error

Despite the ongoing popularity of bullbaiting, there was, by the late 1700s, growing opposition to its practice. In 1802 a bill to abolish bullbaiting was introduced into Parliament, where it was defeated in the House of Commons after fierce debate. One of the prominent defenses of bullbaiting was the argument that beef tasted better and was more tender if the bulls on which it had been grown were exercised in the bullring before being slaughtered. In fact, the old Court Roll of the Manor at Barnard Castle contained the following proscription: "No butcher shall kill any bull two years old [and] upwards, unless he first be brought to the ring and sufficiently halted [baited]."

By 1835, however, it was game over for bullbaiting and other blood sports such as bearbaiting and dogfighting, all of which were outlawed by an act of Parliament. Nevertheless bullbaiting was held now and again in England for roughly 20 more years.

Fun Facts

William De Warren (c.1036–1088), the Earl of Surrey, is often cited as the father of bullbaiting. One day as the earl was standing on a castle wall, he noticed two bulls fighting over a cow in the meadow below. Several of the neighborhood butchers' dogs noticed this fight, too, and they pursued one of the bulls—maddened by the noise and commotion—throughout the town. The earl was so entertained by this activity that he offered to allow the town's butchers perpetual use of the castle meadow for its continuance, as long as they could find a mad bull for baiting six weeks to the day before Christmas.

5

Bulldogs Get a Makeover

With the demise of bullbaiting, the "purebred" Bulldog appeared to have outlived his usefulness. Although he had been described as "the most valiant beast the Almighty (assisted by a number of sadistic breeders) had chosen to create," he was also described as a "devil incarnate."

Fun Facts

The oldest single-breed specialty club is The Bulldog Club (England), which was formed in 1875. Members of this club met frequently at the Blue Post pub on Oxford Street in London, where they wrote the first standard for the breed.

Fortunately there were enough people who admired the Bulldog's valor, tenaciousness, and loyalty—and who believed these qualities well worth preserving. Such was the Bulldog's devotion to his master that he (the Bulldog) might be injured, bleeding, and near death, but if his master ordered him back into the ring, the Bulldog would face his opponent once again without hesitation.

Moreover, when he or she was not raising a ruckus in the bullring, the Bulldog got along quite well with other animals, even bulls. One game female Bulldog, who had pinned the same hulking bull a dozen times in the ring, slept many a night with him in his stall. There, we are told, the two rivals were "as amicable as doves."

One has to love a dog with that kind of attitude, and by 1864 there were enough people in England who did to warrant the establishment of the first Bulldog club, whose motto was "Hold Fast." Sadly this club held fast for only three years before disbanding, but during that time the first Bulldog standard was written in an attempt to describe the ideal member of the breed.

A second Bulldog Club was founded in 1875. It was incorporated in 1894 and has been described as "the forerunner of all dog clubs in the world." One of its chief missions was to promote a moderate size in Bulldogs by discouraging the introduction of Spanish Bulldogs, which often weighed more than 100 pounds (45.5 kg), into English breeding programs. The standard written by this Bulldog club is remarkably similar to the official breed standard today.

The Bulldog in America

Bulldogs were brought to America not only by immigrants seeking their fortunes but also by those whose fortunes already had been made. In the more fortunate group was Sir William Verner, who in 1880 exhibited one of the first Bulldogs shown in United States, a brindle-and-white named Donald.

Six years later the Bulldog was sufficiently established in this country to merit recognition by the American Kennel Club (AKC). Four years after that, in 1890, the Bulldog Club of America (BCA) was founded by H. D. Kendall of Lowell, Massachusetts, who wanted to bring together people interested in "the thoughtful and careful breeding of the English Bulldog in America." At first the BCA adopted the English Bulldog standard, but as this standard was not considered sufficiently descriptive, an executive committee was created in 1896 to draft a new standard.

The Bulldog's popularity in this country continued to grow. In 1915 he ranked fifth among the breeds recognized by the AKC, the highest ranking

Breed Truths

One day in August 1996, in Carrboro, North Carolina, Police Captain John Butler got a call from his wife. "Rock ate a car," she said.

Rock was Butler's three-year-old, 65-pound (29.5-kg), red Bulldog. The car was a blue 1996 Geo, weight undisclosed, being driven by one of Butler's neighbors. Even though Rock had inflicted $1,000 damage on the car with his teeth, Butler did not want people to get the wrong impression about Bulldogs.

"They're big babies," he told the *Chapel Hill Herald*. "They love to be petted. They do stupid, entertaining things."

Butler also assured the *Herald* that Rock had meant the car no harm. "As soon as the guy stopped," said Butler, "Rock stopped chewing on the car because he thought he was going to get a ride. He's not a vicious dog."

Vicious? No. Optimistic? For sure. How many people are going to open the door for a 65-pound dog with his teeth in the quarter panel? Bulldogs must certainly have a keener sense of the absurd than most people do.

the breed has ever held. That ascent was followed eventually by a period of decline, and in 1973 the Bully hit an all-time low of 41 on the AKC's hit parade. Since then the breed has enjoyed a revival that saw it return to the AKC's top 10 in 2008. The following year Bullies were ranked eighth among the 156 breeds registered by the AKC.

Famous Bulldog Mascots

At least 31 institutions of higher learning, roughly 200 institutions of lower and elementary learning, untold businesses, and the United States Marine Corps are known as the "Bulldogs." In fact, the Bulldog was considered an emblem of the United States during World War I.

Whenever somebody is looking for a mascot that personifies toughness, tenacity, durability, and loyalty—just the sort of qualities you want in a school or in a fighting force—the Bully is the go-to breed. Here, in the order in which they were adopted, are the stories of four of those mascots.

Yale University Although most schools represented by a Bulldog are willing to settle for someone in a Bulldog suit, a few are also represented by the real deal. The first of the live Bulldog mascots is Handsome Dan of Yale University.

In 1889 a Yale student named Andrew B. Graves, who played tackle on the school's football team, bought a dog for $5 from a blacksmith in New Haven, Connecticut, where Yale is located. Mr. Graves named the dog Handsome Dan and took him to a football game, an appearance that turned into the custom of leading Dan across the field just before the start of football and baseball games. That custom survives to this day.

One newspaper reporter described Handsome Dan as looking "like a cross between an alligator and a horned frog . . . He was always taken to games on a leash, and the Harvard football team for years owed its continued existence to the fact that the rope held."

In reality, Handsome Dan, who was entirely white, was successful not only as a mascot but also as a show dog. He won hundreds of ribbons, many at the expense of dogs from England.

Handsome Dan died in 1898, the year after he and Mr. Graves had set out on a trip around the world. For many years his stuffed body stood in the old Yale gymnasium. When that was torn down, Handsome Dan was sent to the Peabody Museum for reconstruction. He now lives in a sealed glass case in one of the trophy rooms of Yale's Payne Whitney Gymnasium. Meanwhile, Handsome Dan XVII, who was born March 21, 2007, reigned on the Yale campus at the time of this writing (December 2008).

Mack Trucks Inc. The biggest wheel in corporate circles is the Bulldog that has adorned the front of Mack trucks since 1922. This "Built Like a Mack Truck" image was suggested by a group of satisfied customers— British soldiers in World War I who told Mack company representatives that the blunt-nosed trucks reminded them of Bulldogs as they (the soldiers) made their resolute way through the mud in France carrying supplies to the front.

The United States Marine Corps The Bulldog became the Marines' official mascot on October 14, 1922, when an English Bulldog named King Bulwark was renamed Jiggs and enlisted in the corps for the "term of life" by General Smedley Butler during a formal ceremony at the Quantico, Virginia, Marine base.

Private Jiggs was promoted to corporal within three months. On New Year's Day 1924, Corporal Jiggs was promoted to sergeant. Seven months later he made sergeant major. When he died on January 9, 1927, his satin-lined coffin lay in state in a hangar at Quantico, surrounded by flowers from hundreds of Marine Corps admirers. He was buried with full military honors.

Jiggs II was donated to the corps by his owner, former heavyweight boxing champion Gene Tunney, who had fought with the Marines in France during World War I. The reign of Jiggs II was short. He died of heat exhaustion in 1928 after what was described as "one of his many rampages." Had he lived longer, he might have been drummed out of the corps for biting people and for general insubordination.

From the 1930s through the early 1950s, the Marines' Bulldog mascots were named Smedley, a tribute to General Butler. The mascots' name was changed to "Chesty" in the late 1950s to honor Lieutenant General Lewis B. "Chesty" Puller Jr.

Uga Since 1956 an all-white male Bulldog named Uga (UH-gah) has been the University of Georgia's mascot. Uga I, who reigned for 10 years, begat Uga II, who begat Uga III, and so on. Each Uga—there have been seven to date—was bred, raised, and owned by the Frank W. "Sonny" Seiler family of Savannah, Georgia.

Mr. Seiler was a second-year student at the University of Georgia School of Law in 1956 when he acquired an all-white Bulldog puppy, whom he took to the first Georgia Bulldogs home football game that year. Things just snowballed from there. In addition to Uga, a person in Bulldog drag performs as Hairy Dawg at Georgia Bulldog athletic events, but he need not be the all-white son of his predecessor to get the job.

Uga V (1990–1999) portrayed his father, Uga IV, in the motion picture *Midnight in the Garden of Good and Evil* and was on the cover of *Sports Illustrated* in 1997. The preceding year he made headlines when he lunged at Auburn wide receiver Robert Baker, who had just caught a 21-yard touchdown pass in the Georgia end zone in a November contest. The Georgia Bulldogs hung on to win the game, 56–49, in four overtimes.

Bulldog Pros and Cons

A Bulldog resembles your gruff-looking aunt or uncle, the one who always seemed to be scowling at you but always slipped you some coin when no one was looking. The grumpy expression, wrinkled face, and bowed legs (the Bulldog's) are popular with advertisers who want to give their products a rugged, imposing image; but in spite of his baleful-staring, spike-collar-wearing expression, the Bulldog is a sweetheart, a clown, surprisingly gentle, unshakably loyal, the best friend on four legs that man, woman, child, or marketing department could ever have.

The Bulldog's easygoing disposition makes him perfectly at home in a small house, apartment, or McMansion. His gentle nature and his sensitivity to his people's moods also make him an ideal member of any human pack, especially one that includes small children. What is more, he plays nice with other animals.

A mature Bulldog—one beyond the age of two—appears to be aware of his own power and, as a result, is self-assured and comfortable in his own loose-fitting skin, but his inclination to go along to get along should not be mistaken for a lack of true grit. He is courageous in the extreme, and his devotion to—and sense of responsibility toward—the members of his family make him protective of them. In addition, Bulldogs can be formally polite with strangers, and many Bullies prefer the company of people with whom they are familiar. These traits make the Bulldog an excellent choice for people looking for a family pet *and* protector.

Bulldogs can, nevertheless, be stubborn and mischievous. They are capable of blowing off a command if it conflicts with their agendas. They also will seek—and sometimes demand—the attention they think is their due. In fact, the less attention Bulldogs get, the more inclined they are to amuse themselves, often in ways that are not beneficial to household items or articles of clothing. The trick is to give a Bulldog the attention he needs while letting him know that you are the boss hog. As long as your sense of self and purpose is stronger than his, the two of you will get along well.

For all his hardiness, the Bulldog is prone to breathing difficulties and to drooling. Because his head is shorter—not smaller, but shorter—than that of other dogs, the passages of his salivary glands are shortened. Therefore, when he is excited or hungry, the secretions of those glands overflow their passages and become visible in the form of drool.

The Bulldog Standard

The Bulldog is a smooth-coated, medium-size dog with a heavy, thick-set, low-slung body. His head is gigantic; his face is short; his shoulders are wide; and his legs are sturdy. These features create an imposing image of great stability, vigor, and strength.

The Bulldog skull is watermelon large; its circumference, measured in front of the ears, is at least equal to the height of the Bulldog at his shoulders. The forehead is flat, neither rounded nor domed. The cheeks are well rounded, protruding sideways and outward beyond the eyes.

The Bulldog has small, thin ears set high in the head, as wide apart and as far from the eyes as possible. A Bulldog's ears are not carried erect, but in a "rose" design in which the ear folds inward at its back lower edge, and the upper front edge curves over, outward, and backward, so that part of the inside of the burr is visible.

The Bulldog's eyes are round, moderate in size, and dark in color. Neither sunken nor bulging, they are set low in the skull, as far from the ears as possible and as wide apart as possible, but not so wide that any part of them exceeds the outline of the cheeks.

The temples or frontal bones of the Bulldog are well defined, broad, square, and high. This configuration creates a hollow or groove—known as a "stop"—between the eyes.

The Bulldog's nose is large, broad, and black. Its tip is set back deeply between the eyes. The distance from the bottom of the stop to the tip of the nose is as short as possible and does not exceed the length from the tip of the nose to the edge of the underlip. The nostrils are big, wide, and black, with a well-defined line between them. Any color other than black is considered nonstandard, and a brown or liver-colored nose is cause for disqualification in the show ring, if not in the living room.

The Bulldog's characteristic sour-mug expression is defined by his lips, jaws, and bite. The chops or "flews" are thick, broad, pendant, and deep, completely overhanging the lower jaw at each side. Joining the underlip in front, they cover or nearly cover the teeth, which are scarcely noticeable when the mouth is closed.

The jaws are massive, broad, square, and "undershot," and the upturned lower jaw projects considerably in front of the upper jaw. The teeth are large and strong. The canine teeth or tusks are wide apart, and the six small teeth in front, between the canines, are aligned in an even, level row.

The Bulldog's neck is short, thick, deep, strong, and well arched at the back. There is a slight fall in the back, close behind the shoulders, but from there the spine rises to the loins, the top of which is higher than the top of the shoulders. At the loins the spine curves again suddenly to the tail, forming an arch, which is a distinctive feature of the breed. This configuration is known as a "roach back" or, more precisely, a "wheel back."

The Bulldog has a broad, deep, full chest and a strong, short-backed body that is broad at the shoulders and comparatively narrow at the loins. His shoulders are heavy, muscular, widespread, and outward slanting, projecting the appearance of an immovable object. His front legs are short, stout, straight, muscular, and set wide apart. His calves are well developed and appear bowed in outline, yet his leg bones are not curved or bandy. The feet may be straight or slightly out-turned, but they should not be brought too close together.

The hind legs of the Bulldog are strong, muscular, and longer than the forelegs. The hocks (ankles) should be slightly bent and well let down, giving him length and strength from the loins to the hocks. The lower leg should be short, straight, and strong, with the stifles (knees) turned slightly outward and away from the body. The hocks are thereby made to approach each other, and the hind feet, which are moderate in size, are made to turn well outward.

The Bulldog's tail is either straight or "screwed"—but never curved or curly. It is short and low hung, with an obvious downward carriage, a thick root, and a fine tip. A straight tail is cylindrical and uniformly tapered. A screwed tail exhibits well-defined bends or kinks, which may be abrupt and even knotty, but no portion of the tail should be elevated above the base or root.

Breed Truths

To make dog shows easier to sort out, the AKC assigns dogs to one of eight groups. As of this writing (December 2008) those groups were Sporting, Hound, Working, Terrier, Toy, Non-sporting, Herding, and Miscellaneous, but there may be changes coming eventually in this classification system. The Bulldog is a member of the non-sporting group, a catchall designation for dogs that do not seem to fit in any other category. The non-sporting group is home to 17 breeds ranging from the American Eskimo Dog to the Tibetan Terrier.

The Bulldog has a fine-textured, short coat that is straight, flat, close lying, smooth, and glossy. His skin is soft and loose, especially at the head, neck, and shoulders. His head and face are covered with heavy wrinkles.

The Bulldog is available in various colors. In order of preference they are red brindle, all other brindles, solid white, solid red, fawn or fallow, and piebald (having patches of white and black or other colors).

The Other Bulldogs

There are three other breeds of Bulldogs in addition to the English model. They are the French, the American, and the Olde English bulldogs—although devotees of this last breed prefer "Bulldogge," the Middle English spelling of "Bulldog." The French and American Bulldogs are descended from English Bulldogs that were transported to different countries, where they developed along disparate lines pursuant to the uses to which they were put in their new homes. The Olde English Bulldogge, meanwhile, was created in the United States in the early 1970s by people who wanted to construct a dog with the looks of the eighteenth-century English Bulldog.

French Bulldogs

According to the most prevalent theory of the origin of French Bulldogs, the breed was developed from small English Bulldogs that were taken from England to France in the mid-1800s by Normandy lace workers who went to France seeking work. The diminutive Bullies were by-products of English Bulldog breeding programs. After these dogs had arrived in northern France, they became popular as ratters and family companions in the farming communities where the lace workers had settled. Over time the English imports were crossed with other breeds, most likely the Pug.

As the popularity of the little Bullies spread across France, they caught the fancy of another class of workers—Parisian streetwalkers. This liaison was commemorated on "French postcards" that featured images of half-dressed French prostitutes and their Bouledogues Francais.

Fun Facts

A champion French Bulldog named Gamon de Pycombe, valued at $750 (USD), a significant figure at the time, was aboard the *Titanic* when it sank on April 15, 1912.

The French Bulldog matriculated from the streets of Paris to salons throughout the rest of Europe when the upper classes—whose women, at least, had no truck with prostitutes—adopted the small dogs as a way of showing how daring they (members of the upper classes) could be.

Eventually the French Bulldog found his way to America, where in 1898 the first French Bulldog club was founded. Members of this club as well as other American fanciers of the French Bulldog insisted that the "bat" ear was to be preferred to the "rose" or folded ear of the English Bulldog. Ever since, the French Bulldog has resembled a miniature English Bulldog with bat ears.

American Bulldogs

Many Bulldogs arrived in the United States with working-class immigrants from the British West Midlands who settled in the American South, where they used their dogs for hunting, guard duty, gambling, sport, and ridding the South of feral pigs. Being at some remove from the motherland and the

FYI: Bulldog Breed Comparisons

	Bulldog	French Bulldog	American Bulldog	Old English Bulldogge
Height at Withers	12 to 14 inches (30.5–35.6 cm)	Roughly 12 inches (30.5 cm)	20 to 27 inches (50.8–68.6 cm)	17 to 20 inches (43.2–50.8 cm), depending on sex of dog
Weight Males	50 to 55 pounds (22.7–24.9 kg)	Not to exceed 28 pounds (12.7 kg)*	75 to 125 pounds (34–56.7 kg)	65 to 85 pounds (29.5–39.6 kg)
Weight Females	40 to 45 pounds (18.1–20.4 kg)	Not to exceed 28 pounds (12.7 kg)*	60 to 100 pounds (27.2–45.4 kg)	50 to 70 pounds (22.7–31.8 kg)

*Unisex standard applies to males and females.

dog fancy in either country, the American Bulldogs continued to resemble the English Bulldog of the eighteenth and early nineteenth centuries.

By the end of World War II the American Bulldog was nearly extinct. Efforts to preserve the breed by seeking out and breeding with representatives—and more than a few near representatives—of the breed ultimately resulted in its recognition by the United Kennel Club on January 1, 1999. The breed is not recognized by the AKC.

Olde English Bulldogges

This breed was constructed to resemble the original English bullbaiting dogs of the late eighteenth and early nineteenth centuries. That quest began in 1971 when David Leavitt of Coatesville, Pennsylvania, decided to create a dog with the look, health, and athleticism of English bullbaiting dogs. The original composition of the Olde English Bulldogge was roughly one-half Bulldog, one-sixth Bullmastiff, one-sixth American Pit Bull Terrier, and one-sixth American Bulldog. Mr. Leavitt later formed the Olde English Bulldogge Association to maintain a studbook for the breed and to issue registration papers for Olde English Bulldogges, which are not recognized by the AKC.

Olde English Bulldogge breeders maintain that their breed is free of most of the genetic problems that dog modern-day English Bulldogs. The goal of all Bulldogge breeders is a free-breathing, free-breeding, and free-whelping dog. A worthy goal, indeed.

Chapter Two

The Mind of the Bulldog

There are few sights more amusing than that of a Bulldog playing with a bowling ball by the light of a full moon on a crisp fall night. What a marvelous night for a moon dance, eh Mr. Bully? The gravel in the driveway goes crunch, crunch, crunch as the Bully nudges the ball forward, then pounces on it as though it were an errant toy bent on making its get-away, which, in his mind, it is.

A bowling ball is not the kind of toy you expect to find most dogs playing with, but Bulldogs are not most dogs. They are a breed, a law, and an amusement park unto themselves. "Large and in charge" is the Bully's motto.

The Bulldog's Five Senses

A Bulldog's senses—and his ability to communicate—are functioning at near-adult capacity by the time he is four weeks old. He is fully capable of interacting socially with other dogs and with people by that time, and by the time he comes to your house, at 10 to 12 weeks of age, he is not really a puppy but a little dog in disguise. He experiences the world through senses that are similar to and yet vastly different from ours. It should be no surprise, then, that even though we feel the same, we see things from a different point of view.

Breed Truths

Smell

The human brain is dominated by the visual cortex, whereas the dog brain is dominated by the olfactory cortex. Relative to brain size, the olfactory bulb in dogs is roughly 40 times bigger than it is in humans.

A dog's nose is also rich in mucus. The surface area of a dog's nasal membranes— if you took the time to unfold them and to

When a dog breathes normally, air does not pass directly over his scent receptors, which are near the back of his nose; but if he puts his nose to the grindstone, as it were, and takes a number of shallow sniffs, the air drawn into his nose triggers those receptors, returning more hits than a Google search.

spread them out carefully—is roughly equal to the size of a handkerchief. Do the same with your own nasal membranes and you will wind up with a postage stamp for your efforts.

Not surprisingly, the 5 million primary receptor cells in the human nose are mocked by the 125 to 300 million primary receptor cells in a dog's nose, depending on his breed. That is why dogs can sense odors at concentrations nearly 100 million times lower than humans can—a drop of blood in 5 quarts (4.75 L) of water, for example.

Because breeds with longer noses have the best sense of smell, Bulldogs and other brachycephalic (short-face) breeds are closer to the 125-million-primary-receptor-cell floor than they are to the 300-million-cell ceiling. Nevertheless, their sense of smell is way superior to ours.

Taste

Bulldog owners discover quickly that their dogs are not particular about what they put into their mouths—which makes them great trash compactors. Part of a Bully's willingness to scarf up almost anything results from his relative lack of taste buds, not from his lack of taste. Dogs have fewer taste buds, approximately 1,700, than we humans, who have roughly 9,000. Moreover, a dog's taste buds are clustered near the tip of his tongue, the area on which food spends the least amount of time—or no time at all.

A dog makes up for his lack of taste buds with a well-developed vomeronasal organ, a chemosensory device also known as Jacobson's organ in honor of a Danish physician. Located above the roof of the mouth behind the upper incisors, the vomeronasal organ contains olfactory epithelium that enable a Bully to "taste" smells and to send that information to the limbic system of the brain, the seat of many emotional responses. For this reason Bulldogs are said to enjoy food because of the way it smells, rather than the way it tastes. They are able to make this distinction because the olfactory receptors in the nasal cavity are anatomically distinct from those in Dr. Jacobson's organ.

Because a dog is guided more by his sense of smell than his sense of taste, he will eat, even if he is unwell, as long as he can smell his food. This is why we feed sick Bullies with strong-smelling or strongly seasoned foods or with food that has been warmed slightly in the microwave to boost its flavor.

Hearing

If you want to know the difference between a dog's ability to hear and yours, put on a pair of earmuffs and talk to someone on the phone. Just about anything we can hear, a dog can hear better. In addition, a dog can detect fainter sounds from greater distances, up to four times as great, than we can, and on much higher frequencies.

A dog's frequency range is approximately 40 Hz to 60,000 Hz, a Hz (hertz) being one cycle (sound vibration) per second. The human frequency range is 20 Hz to 20,000 Hz. We may outperform dogs in the detection of low, rumbling bass notes oozing from a car stereo two traffic lights behind us, but dogs box our ears at the other end of the audio spectrum. (A dog's hearing is keen enough to detect a mouse singing falsetto half a mile away.) Furthermore, dogs are able to determine the direction a sound is coming from much more accurately than we can, and they can differentiate between similar sounds better than we can, too.

Dogs also are able to locate and to capture sound more efficiently than we can because they possess 18 or so muscles that enable them to swivel, tilt, ratchet, raise, or lower their ears to hone in on a sound. As usual, a Bulldog's conformation puts him up against it in hearing contests with other dogs because breeds with erect ears hear better than those with floppy ones.

Touch

Touch is the first sense that a dog develops. Mothers begin touching their puppies almost immediately after they are born. Puppies, for their part,

literally thrive on their mothers' licking and nuzzling, and the comfort they derive from contact during infancy leads them to seek contact with other dogs and with humans throughout life. In fact, touch can have a calming effect on a dog's heart rate, as it can on ours.

Breed Truths

A dog's visual acuity, the ability to see details, is roughly six times poorer than the average human's. Acuity, which is measured in cycles per degree, is an assessment of the number of lines that can be seen as distinct entities in the visual field. Humans can see approximately 30 cycles per degree, whereas dogs can see roughly 12.

A Bully's sense of touch is facilitated by touch-sensitive hairs called vibrissae, which are capable of sensing airflow. Vibrissae develop above the eyes, on the muzzle, and below the jaws. In addition, a dog's entire body, including his paws, is covered with touch-sensitive nerve endings.

Although body sensitivity varies among dogs, most enjoy being petted around the head, chest, back, and—if they roll over onto their backs as you are petting them—on their bellies as well. The most sensitive nerve endings are found along the spine and toward the tail.

Touch is actually a confederation of different somatic senses: the sensations of temperature, pressure, and pain; kinesthetic senses that give a Bully a conception of his body in space; and visceral senses such as stomachaches or nausea.

Sight

The retina of a dog's eye is lined with rods and cones, just as it is in humans. Rods are much more prevalent than cones are in both species, but even more so in dogs. Rods work best in low light and in the detection of motion. That is why dogs see better at night than we do.

The central retina of the canine eye contains roughly 20 percent cones. In humans, however, there is an area called the fovea, which is all cones all the time. Cones work best in mid to high levels of light; they also are capable of detecting color. The fovea is further responsible for the sharp central vision necessary when we read, watch television or movies, and drive—activities in which a Bully may have an interest but does not need to participate actively.

According to perceived wisdom, dogs are color-blind, and for once perceived wisdom appears to be correct, to an extent. The average dog's color vision is similar to that of a human deuteranope, a person that is red-green colorblind.

PERSONALITY POINTERS
Bulldog Body Language

Bulldog Mood	Friendly	Curious or Excited	Playful
Head Carriage	Normal posture and head position	Normal posture and head position	"Play bow," chest and head lowered to ground, head looking up
Eyes	Open normally	Open normally	Open normally
Ears	Normal carriage	Normal carriage	Normal carriage
Mouth	Closed or relaxed	Open, teeth covered with lips, may pant	Closed or slightly open
Body	Relaxed posture or wiggling with excitement	Still and observant or animated	Chest lowered to ground, rump elevated
Tail	Most Bulldogs wag their entire back ends instead of their tails, which were not built for wagging	Most Bulldogs wag their entire back ends instead of their tails, which were not built for wagging	Most Bulldogs wag their entire back ends instead of their tails, which were not built for wagging

In tests conducted at the University of California, Santa Barbara, researchers concluded that dogs actually do see colors, but not so many as we normally do. Whereas our rainbows are violet, blue, blue-green, green, yellow, orange, and red, our Bullies' rainbows are dark blue, light blue, gray, light yellow, darker yellow (close to brown), and dark gray. In short, a Bully's world consists of yellows, blues, and grays. What we perceive as red appears as yellow to a dog, and anything that is green to us is light brown to white to him. Therefore, the grass is not always greener on the other side to a Bully. It is, rather, a tanner shade of pale.

Although many humans would be freaked out at the prospect of their lawns looking brownish, dogs are not at a disadvantage for not being able to see all the colors of the spectrum. During the course of evolution dogs and humans each developed the visual system that worked best for them. Until we domesticated them, dogs were not diurnal (of/or belonging to the daytime). The ability

Apprehensive or Anxious	Fearful	Subordinate
Neck stiff, head may be pulled back slightly	Head slightly lowered	Head slightly lowered
Open slightly wider than normal, whites of eyes may be visible more than usual, may have fixed stare	Open slightly wider than normal, whites of eyes may be visible more than usual, may have fixed stare	Eyes partially closed
Pulled slightly back	Pulled slightly back or held closer to the skull than usual	Pulled slightly back or held closer to the skull than usual
Closed or slightly open in a tight "grin" with teeth showing	Slightly open, teeth may be visible, may be drooling	Lips of mouth pulled back in "grin," may lick or nuzzle
Tense	Tense, trembling, may take a position poised to run, may release anal sac contents in fear	May roll over on back and expose belly, may also dribble urine in submission
Not wagging to be sure, but not noticeably lowered either as the tail is short and carried low already	Not a good indicator because Bullies' tails do not reach between their legs	Not a good indicator because Bullies' tails do not reach between their legs

to see at night was far more important to the dog than the ability to detect color. Their prey is often camouflaged by its surroundings, so dogs are unable to rely on color vision cues as heavily as humans do to find their prey, which is usually hidden in plain view on brightly lit supermarket shelves.

Another reason that dogs see much better at night than humans do is the mirror-like tissue in dogs' eyes. This tissue enhances night vision by reflecting incoming light back through the retina, re-stimulating the eyes' light-sensing cells and boosting their signal to the brain. You can demonstrate the effect of this mirror-like tissue by shining a flashlight in your Bully's eyes at night. The reflected light gleaming back at you is known as "eyeshine."

Dogs have a wider field of view than humans do and a better ability to detect motion at the horizon. A dog can recognize moving objects nearly half a mile (0.8 km) away, while humans often fail to see that the car in front of them has stopped to make a left-hand turn.

Bullbaiting and the Bulldog Mind-Set

When people discuss the effects of bullbaiting on Bulldogs, they usually talk about the breed's conformation: its wide shoulders, its short forelegs, its jutting lower jaw, its facial wrinkles, its loose skin; but bullbaiting left an imprint on the Bulldog's character as well. Bullbaiting burnished to a fare-thee-well the valor, loyalty, and absolute devotion to their masters for which Bulldogs are known and loved today. The rigors of bullbaiting also shaped the Bulldog into a dog that is not demanding. Unfortunately bullbaiting perfected the stubbornness that can make Bulldogs resist doing anything they do not see a good reason for doing.

Bulldogs have a reputation for not being terribly bright. It is a reputation that is unfair and unfounded, but somewhat understandable. It is difficult to look that gnarly and to look intelligent at the same time.

If your definition of intelligence includes mother wit and guile, Bulldogs are valedictorian material. For example, they are masters of the guilt trip. They know that humans are suckers for a sad face or a well-timed sigh.

How Bulldogs Experience Humans

Bulldogs know more about us than they let on. They may not write human-training manuals, but they read us like books nonetheless. Here are the fruits of their observations, expressed in syntax as near to a Bully's as possible, that is, with a disregard for the subjects of sentences and a tendency to speak of themselves in the third person.

Indulgent Owners

These owners allow their Bully to do whatever he wants for fear that asking him to behave—never mind telling him to—will break his spirit or cause him not to love them. But, they wind up with a hyperactive, out-of-control dog who does not love them anyway, because who loves a doormat? Bulldogs look up to leaders; Bulldogs look down on doormats.

The Unpredictable Owner

Owners who never react the same way twice from day to day—and some days from one hour to the next—are unpredictable. Jump into her lap today, cool, she is wearing jeans and just got finished gardening. But, jump into her lap tomorrow when she just gets home from work and has not had time to change her clothes yet—all hell breaks loose. These owners cannot decide whether to allow the Bully to sleep on the sofa or not, then finally decide he is allowed to sleep on the sofa if his feet are clean. What do Bulldogs know from clean feet or from unpredictable owners?

The Absentee Owner

Absentee owners are seldom home except when they are sleeping. How do they expect to have the time to teach a Bulldog all the things he needs to know? If they had a clue, they would find Bully a better home instead of this glorified motel and get a Chia pet—or get Bully a playmate, either a two-legged one who comes around to walk him several times a day, or a four-legged one whom Bully can train himself. These owners have the nerve to expect a Bulldog to be loving and well behaved, because in the end, the love you take is equal to the love you make.

The Contrite Owner

Contrite owners are abseentee owners on a guilt trip, which usually makes matters even worse. One day they have only a hour to spend with their Bulldog, but the next day, they follow their Bulldog around and even make him something fabulous to eat. Then, it's back to dry kibble again—if they even remember to feed their Bulldog at all.

The other kind of contrite owner is the one who whacked Bully with a rolled-up newspaper yesterday when he peed on the throw rug in the den, and then lets him sleep in the bed with her today. Tomorrow he will be back in the kitchen. Confusing? You betcha!

Communicating with Your Bulldog

Voice Although Bulldogs can accumulate a significant working vocabulary—which, unfortunately, often excludes the words *no, off, cut it out,* or *darn it*—we communicate with them more through tone of voice and volume than through dictionary meanings. If, for example, we say, *"Etslay ogay, oybay"* in a bright, cheery tone when we get Bully's leash, he is going to react with the same enthusiasm as if we had said, *"Let's go, boy"*; but if we say, *"Let's go, boy"* in the stern, disapproving tone we use to say *"Stop"* when we find him devouring the new *Rolling Stone,* he is apt to cringe instead. If you want to teach your Bully the meaning of a word or phrase, chain it with an action. If you say, *"Let's go out, Sport"* before getting your boy's leash, in relatively short order all you have to do is say, *"Let's go out, Sport"* and he is off the couch and heading for the door. If you want to impress your friends, teach Bully to respond to a question: *"Wanna go out, boy?"* Sooner or later someone is sure to exclaim, "It's almost like he knows what you're saying." Duh!

You can also put your Bully's capacity for distinguishing pitch to other uses. Because dogs respond most quickly to sharp sounds—actually that should be "more quickly" in the case of Bulldogs—add a few hand claps or a brisk whistle to reinforce your voice command when you are teaching him to come when you call. Commands such as *"Stop"* should always be given in a sharper tone than you would use if you wanted to praise your dog.

Hands Most if not all Bulldog puppies see hands as something on which to chew. Eventually they associate hands with other functions: petting, food delivery, grooming, and taking stuff out of their mouths. They are, accordingly, disposed to viewing human hands as their 10-fingered friends. We let our fingers do the talking whenever we touch our Bullies. That talking should be done in a gentle tone of voice, one that communicates loving kindness. If we use our hands to communicate displeasure—either implied or inflicted—our dogs are likely to become hand shy, i.e., to crouch warily if someone tries to pet them.

Truth be told, dog behavior experts are of two minds on the subject of hand corrections. Some behavior experts and dog writers rank hand corrections right up there with child abuse, but others say it is not the use of hands but the way in which we use them that does harm. These experts teach restraint in the use of hands—a quick, light "pop" under the chin or a soft but noticeable jab in the shoulders with the fingers of one hand held straight and pointing in the shoulder's direction. These experts also caution against ever striking a dog from above or behind. If you follow their guidelines, you can use hand corrections when he is being truly obnoxious without worrying about traumatizing him.

Facial Expressions

Persons who believe that dogs can "sense our moods" may have to rethink that theory. According to the findings of a study reported in the October 2008 edition of *New Scientist*, dogs do not read our emotions, they read the teleprompters on which our emotions are written—our faces.

The study, led by Dr. Kin Guo of the University of Lincoln (United Kingdom), was based on a phenomenon called "left gaze bias." Before this study, research had demonstrated that owing to differences between the two hemispheres of the brain, human faces are lopsided when it comes to displaying emotion. The right side of the face, which is controlled by the left side of the brain, more clearly expresses emotion because emotion is the province of the brain's left side. Meanwhile, the left side of the human face, controlled by the buttoned-down right side of the brain, is more devoid of emotion. Therefore, when we meet someone, we tend to direct our attention to the left (the other person's right side) because that is where the clues to that person's emotional state are displayed. The researchers found that dogs do the same thing when they look at people.

The 17 dogs that participated in the study were shown images of human faces, dog faces, monkey faces, and inanimate objects. Each dog's eye and head movements were videotaped as he looked at the images. An analysis of the tapes revealed that the dogs' head and eye movements suggested that they recognized the human faces and that their eyes drifted left when looking at them just as our eyes do when we meet someone. Interestingly the dogs in the study did not look left when they were shown images of animals or inanimate objects. Dr. Guo theorized that over thousands of generations of association with humans, dogs may have evolved left gaze bias as a way to gauge our emotions. He had nothing to say about what dogs do when they meet two-faced people.

Body Language

Although scientists are still struggling to figure out why dogs have the ability to read human body language, Bulldog owners could tell them that dogs operate on the theory that our movements and gestures reveal much about what we are going to do next, and if it involves them, they are on the case. That is why if we are sitting in the kitchen and cast an eye toward the rack where Bully's leash is hanging, he is at the door.

Bulldogs also are able to read displeasure in our body movements, and we should turn that ability to our advantage. If your Bulldog puppy begins jumping up and putting his paws on you by way of greeting when you return home, simply turn and walk away without acknowledging him. Eventually when you return home, he will manage his enthusiasm better.

Chapter Three

How to Choose
a Bulldog

After you have decided that life is not worth living without a Bulldog, there still are other decisions to be made: Where is the best place to acquire a Bulldog? How much does a Bully cost? Does a male or a female make a better pet? Is a puppy, an adolescent, or an adult the best choice for you? Does color make a difference? How can you tell if a puppy has a sound mind in a sound body?

Where to Find a Bulldog

Bulldog puppies are all wide eyes, flapping ears, and heavy breathing. They are soft, cute, klutzy, and energetic. They can make you smile when you do not feel like smiling, and they can wring a chuckle out of you on the most cheerless days. Bullies are always ready to assist at nap time, mealtime, bedtime, and all the other times of our lives. They are matchless at keeping secrets, at keeping us amused, and at keeping loneliness at bay. Dogs even have been credited with lowering our blood pressure and increasing our life spans.

Given those talents, Bulldogs ought to be in great demand, and they are. Between 1997 and 2008, Bullies climbed from twenty-sixth to eighth in popularity among the breeds registered by the American Kennel Club (AKC). No other breed in the AKC's top 20 made that kind of progress during the same period.

Breeder

The best person from whom to buy a Bulldog is a "reputable breeder" who raises a few well-socialized litters each year. Such an individual is often, though not always, involved in showing Bulldogs, and the term *reputable breeder* should not be conferred automatically on someone just because he or she is breeding for the show ring. The defining word here is *few*: The fewer puppies a breeder raises, the more time he or she has to socialize them properly.

Most reputable Bulldog breeders belong to the Bulldog Club of America, and that is the best place to start looking for a breeder. The breeder referral page of the club's website, *thebca.org/breedref.html*, contains a list of breeders organized by division and by states within each division. The breeders listed by the BCA have been approved by the board of governors of their respective division. A listing by the BCA does not, however, "constitute any endorsement" by the club.

Bulldog breeders may advertise in dog magazines, in the classified sections of newspapers, on bulletin boards in veterinary offices, in grooming shops and feed stores, and in *The Bulldogger*, a publication no Bulldog lover should be without (see "Resources," page 179). Bulldog breeders also can be found through the breeder classifieds section of the American Kennel Club's website, *www.akc.org/classified/index.cfm*, and at dog shows, which are advertised in newspapers, veterinarians' offices, dog magazines, and, occasionally, on television.

If your search for a Bulldog leads you to a dog show, be sure to buy a catalog, which contains the names and addresses of all the people who have dogs entered in that show.

Pet Store

If you consider buying a Bulldog from a pet store, you should ask the salesperson who deposits a puppy in your arms for the name, address, and phone number of the puppy's breeder. If the salesperson is unable to provide that information, you should proceed with caution, because you are proceeding with less information about the puppy than you would have if you were buying from a breeder.

If the pet store provides the name and address of the puppy's breeder—and if that person lives nearby—contact the breeder and arrange a visit so that you can observe the conditions in which the puppy was raised and ask any questions you might have about the puppy.

CAUTION

Most people are eager to take their new Bulldog puppies home as soon as possible, but reputable breeders do not let them go until they are at least 10 weeks old. By that age a puppy has been weaned, is eating solid food, and, believe it or not, has begun the journey to adulthood, though his roadmap may have food stains and teeth marks all over it.

Puppies younger than 10 weeks of age are still babies. If they are taken from their mothers and their siblings, the stress of adjusting to new surroundings could make puppies sick or difficult to housetrain. Puppies taken from the nest too soon may compensate by nursing on blankets, sofa cushions, or other objects you do not want them chewing—a habit they may keep the rest of their lives.

Nevertheless, some breeders, especially those with too many puppies underfoot, are eager to place puppies as quickly as possible. Do not let anyone talk you into taking a puppy before he is 10 weeks old, no matter how "mature for his age" that puppy might be.

If the breeder lives far away, you should telephone to ask any questions about the puppy that the salesperson in the pet store might not be able to answer: How many other puppies were in the litter? How old was the puppy when he left his mother? How many dogs does the breeder have? How many litters do those dogs produce in a year? How many different breeds of puppies does the breeder produce? Why does the breeder choose to sell to pet stores rather than directly to the public?

You also may want to call the animal shelter or Better Business Bureau in the town where the breeder lives to ask if the breeder enjoys a good reputation in the community. In fact, you should make this inquiry if you buy a Bulldog directly from a breeder. No matter where you purchase a Bulldog, you should find out as much as possible about his background.

Helpful Hints

In your search for a Bulldog, do not overlook Bullies that already belong to somebody. Visit dog parks, farmers' markets, outdoor cafés, and any other places where people and their dogs can be found taking the air. Chat up Bulldog owners. Ask them where they got their dogs and if they would get another dog from that individual or organization.

Animal Shelter

It is difficult to imagine that anyone would be unhappy with a Bulldog. Such moral deficiency boggles the mind. Nevertheless, some Bulldogs, through no fault of their own, are not the sunshine in their owners' lives. In that case the owner should return the Bulldog to his breeder, who should take the dog

FYI: OFA Certification

Bulldogs have one of the highest incidences of hip dysplasia of any breed. According to the Orthopedic Foundation for Animals (OFA), an organization that tests canine hips and elbows for genetic defects such as hip dysplasia, 74 percent of the 410 Bullies tested from January 1974 through December 2007 were dysplastic.

Because this condition is so common among Bulldogs, you should not buy a puppy from anyone who has not had that puppy's parents X-rayed to check for signs of hip dysplasia. Those X-rays, which can be taken by most veterinarians, are submitted to the OFA for reading and analysis. The OFA then issues a certificate for each dog based on its reading of that dog's X-rays. Dogs that are rated "excellent" are recommended for breeding; dogs rated "good" are classified suitable for breeding; and those that are rated "fair" can be used for breeding, although the OFA does not recommend doing so.

If the breeder has some excuse for not getting the parents certified—"Oh, they were not old enough yet"—take your checkbook elsewhere. No one should breed two dogs without knowing if they are at risk for producing dysplastic puppies.

The same advice applies if the person from whom you are interested in buying a Bulldog has not bothered to have that dog's parents certified free of known heritable eye diseases by the Canine Eye Registration Foundation.

back and find him another, more suitable home—or look after the dog forever, as all reputable breeders are apt to do.

Unfortunately, not all breeders—and no pet stores—will welcome back a 15-month-old Bulldog "because he just doesn't get along with our old cat." Therefore, some Bulldogs wind up in animal shelters with their tails tucked between their legs, as far as that maneuver is possible. If you are willing to wait for a Bulldog until one is surrendered at a shelter, visit a shelter and ask to be put on its waiting list.

Bulldog Rescue Organizations

Bulldog rescue organizations exist to find second (and sometimes third) homes for Bulldogs whose first homes did not turn out to be ideal. Members of rescue clubs often cooperate with animal shelters by providing foster homes for lost, abandoned, or surrendered Bulldogs until suitable new owners can be located. Bulldog rescue groups generally maintain websites from which you can download an adoption form and read the histories of Bullies that are—or soon will be—available for adoption. Animal shelters may be able to refer you to a Bulldog rescue group in your area, but if not, visit the website of the Bulldog Club of America Rescue Network, *www.rescuebulldogs.org.*

A good rescue club will ask you a lot of questions and may want to visit your house to see whether it is Bulldog worthy. You should also expect to make a donation to the group. The amount will vary from group to group, and may reach as high as $400 or more if the Bully you want to adopt has needed medical attention.

The Choice Is Yours

Your reason for wanting a Bulldog may influence your choice of a puppy. If you are interested in showing, for example, you will have to pay more attention to physical characteristics than you would otherwise. If you are looking solely for a companion, as most people are, you still will have to decide whether age, sex, color, cost—and maybe even a second puppy—will figure into your decision.

Breeding or Showing

Breeding a handsome, well-mannered Bulldog can provide joy, satisfaction, and the feeling of achievement that accompanies any creative effort. There is, however, some responsibility attached to this undertaking. If you are thinking about buying a puppy for breeding, ask yourself why you want to do so. If your answers include winning fame and fortune in the dog world, you most likely are going to be disappointed. Few breeders become overnight sensations, few litters are filled with nothing but show-quality

puppies, and fewer people make money selling puppies. Indeed, making money is not a valid reason for breeding Bulldogs.

Sex

Some people—for reasons of personal choice, experience, or both—prefer the company of male or female dogs. Any Bulldog, given attention, a supply of things to chew, and a place on the bed at night, will make an excellent companion. Nevertheless, some people claim that females are "high strung" or that males are "aggressive." These canine experts generally do not base their conclusions on a large sample of dogs they have studied. They usually are talking about a few dogs they have known from limited experience.

One can say for certain that spaying a female Bulldog will cost $50 or so more than neutering a male. Otherwise there is no difference in the expense associated with housing an altered male or female—and no difference in the amount of care each sex requires.

Age

Bulldog puppies could not be more appealing. They are a triumph of curiosity over common sense; what they lack in experience they make up in exuberance. They barge joyfully through their food bowls and their owners' lives. Bullies are a snuffling bouquet of puppy breath, a tail-wagging, head-lolling, eyes-shining experience. They make the most poker-faced individuals laugh and inspire the most proper folks to engage in embarrassing fits of baby talk. The less controlled among us are, of course, toast.

The adolescent Bulldog is scarcely less appealing than his younger self, and an adult Bulldog is not much different from an adolescent. Indeed, it is difficult to determine where adolescence leaves off and adulthood begins with Bulldogs. Therefore, the prospective owner should not feel as if he or she *has* to have a puppy. A Bulldog of any age is a dog for all seasons.

Color

As we have seen in Chapter 1 (page 13), the "preferred" Bulldog colors, according to the AKC Bulldog standard, are "red brindle, all other brindles, solid white, solid red, fawn or fallow, and piebald (having patches of white and black or other colors).

"A perfect piebald is preferable to a muddy brindle or defective solid color," the standard continues. "Solid black is very undesirable, but not so objectionable if occurring to a moderate degree in piebald patches. The brindles to be perfect should have a fine, even, and equal distribution of the composite colors. In brindles and solid colors a small white patch on the chest is not considered detrimental. In piebalds the color patches should be well defined, of pure color and symmetrically distributed."

If reading that does not make your eyes tired, one cannot imagine what would. If you are going to show your dog, you have to pay attention to such details. Otherwise, any color you like is a perfectly good color for a Bulldog.

Breed Truths

Unless you are planning to show your Bulldog or to breed him, you want a pet-quality Bulldog. Despite its bargain-basement sound, "pet-quality" simply means that a dog has some cosmetic liability that argues against his breeding or showing success.

Pet-quality Bulldogs may not possess quite the right color, or they may have muzzles that are too narrow, ears that are too erect, tails that are curved or curly, or some other "fault" or minor constellation of faults. All the above are surface defects. They do not in any way detract from the Bulldog's matchless personality. You cannot judge a Bulldog by its cover. Every Bulldog is a high-quality dog on the inside.

Cost

Age, quality, supply, demand, and geography collaborate to determine the price of a Bulldog. Very young Bullies, 12 weeks old or so, are generally priced between $1,500 and $2,000, and sometimes higher, depending on the breeder's opinion of their potential. A $1,500 puppy, though his ears may not be correct and his tail may be curved, will make a fine companion if he is healthy and is properly socialized. The same is true of a $5,000 puppy, whose higher price tag reflects the fact that his breeder believes he has some show potential.

One Dog or Two

If you have no other pets and your house is empty during the day, you might consider getting two Bulldogs. In addition to human company, puppies should enjoy the company of another dog, who will always be interested in romping and stomping long after humans have tired of the game, and who is always more willing than a human is to let a dog use him as a pillow.

If buying a second Bully would tax your budget, adopt a dog—one that is roughly the same age as the Bulldog you are purchasing—from a local shelter. Watching two dogs at play is at least twice as much fun as watching only one. Besides, if your Bully has a playmate, you will not be required to fill that role so often. Also, your dogs will be less apt to get bored or lonely if they have company when you are not at home.

If you have a dog already and that dog is still of flexible age, preferably five years old or younger, it is not too late to add a second dog to the household, providing you manage the introduction properly. (See "Bulldogs and Other Pets," page 63.) Before you do, though, you should consider certain realities.

Two dogs are not as easy to keep, feed, clean, and look after as one; nor, in some cases, will you simply be doubling your workload by adding a second Bully. That load can increase geometrically, not linearly, depending on the personalities of the dogs involved, but whether or not your workload increases by a factor of two or three, the pleasure that two dogs provides is always more than twice as great as the pleasure that one provides.

Selecting a Healthy Puppy

A healthy puppy has eyes that are shiny, bright, and clear; a nose that is cool and slightly damp; gums that are neither pale nor inflamed; and ears that are free of wax or dirt. His body is smooth, perhaps a little plump, but not skinny. His coat is free of bald patches, scabs, or specks of black dirt. The area around his tail is free of moisture, dirt, or discoloration.

A puppy with teary eyes may be in poor health—especially if his nose is warm or dry. Pale gums may be a sign of anemia; a puppy with inflamed gums may have gingivitis. Wax in a puppy's ears might simply be a sign of neglect, but ears with caked-on dirt may be infested with ear mites. If a puppy's ribs are sticking out or if he is potbellied, he may be undernourished or have worms.

A puppy with a dull coat or a coat dotted with scabs, specks of dirt, or bald spots may have ringworm or fleas. A puppy whose hindquarters are wet may develop urine scalding. Dirty hindquarters may be a sign of diarrhea. Both urine scalding and diarrhea are signs of potential poor health.

Basic Personality Test

The basic, do-it-yourself puppy personality test consists of wiggling a few fingers along the floor about 6 inches (15 cm) in front of a puppy or waving a small toy back and forth about the same distance away. Any puppy that responds to either of these tests by waddling over to investigate you is a good bet to make a fine companion. An even better bet is the puppy that rushes over to investigate you before you have a chance to start wiggling your fingers.

CHECKLIST

The Healthy Puppy

	Positive Signs	Troublesome Signs
Eyes	☐ Shiny, bright, clear	☐ Teary, bloodshot, caked
Nose	☐ Cool, slightly damp	☐ Warm, dry, caked
Gums	☐ Pink	☐ Pale, inflamed
Ears	☐ Clean	☐ Wax, dirt, ear mite debris
Body	☐ Soft, slightly plump	☐ Emaciated or potbellied
Coat	☐ Clean and smooth	☐ Bald patches, scabs, flea dirt
Tail Area	☐ Clean, dry	☐ Wet or crusty with dried diarrhea

Well-adjusted, healthy puppies are curious about fingers, toys, and anything else within sight that moves. Nervous or timid puppies, or those that are not feeling well, are more cautious. Poorly adjusted puppies shrink from new phenomena.

If you have other pets or children at home, the inquisitive puppy is the best choice. The bashful puppy might well make a fine companion, too, but he may take longer to adjust, and is, perhaps, better left for experienced dog owners who currently are without pets or young children.

And the shy puppy? Shy puppies need love, too, in spades. If you have no other pets or if you plan to acquire two puppies at once and you have the time and patience required to nurture such a reluctant violet, you may be the person this puppy needs. If not, perhaps the next person who comes along will be the right owner for this needful pup.

Although temperament is heritable to some degree, the way a puppy is raised is more important in shaping his personality. Bulldogs that are not handled often enough between the ages of three and twelve weeks are less likely to develop into well-adjusted family members than puppies who receive frequent handling and attention during that period. Therefore, you should ask how many litters a breeder produces each year and how many other litters he or she was raising when your puppy was growing up.

A breeder who produces more than four litters a year—or who was raising three or four other litters while your puppy's litter was maturing— may not have had time to socialize every puppy in those litters properly. A breeder who raises one or, at most, two litters at a time has more opportunity to give each of those puppies the individual attention he or she deserves. In general, the fewer puppies a breeder produces, the more user-friendly those puppies will be.

CAUTION

Anemia in Bulldogs is caused by the excessive loss—or the inadequate production—of red blood cells. Symptoms of anemia include white or pale gums, weakness, and a fast pulse. Anemia caused by blood loss can be treated with a diet rich in iron, protein, and vitamin B12.

Chronic iron deficiency is a clear indication of insidious loss of blood—a condition commonly caused by wounds or parasites such as worms and fleas. Sometimes, however, anemia indicates a more serious illness such as a toxic reaction to a drug.

Contracts, Papers, and Health Certificates

When you buy a puppy, you should receive a sales contract from the puppy's breeder. That contract should specify, among other things, the price of the puppy, the amount of the deposit required to hold the puppy, if any, and when the balance of the payment is due. Most contracts also contain a provision stipulating that if at any time the buyer no longer can keep the puppy—or no longer wishes to keep him—the breeder must be given an

opportunity to buy the puppy back "at the going price for Bulldogs at the time of resale." In addition, if a puppy is not going to be shown or used for breeding, the contract may contain a clause requiring that the puppy be altered when he is old enough.

Finally, a contract should specify that you have a reasonable amount of time—three to five working days after receiving the puppy—in which to take him to a veterinarian to be examined. If the veterinarian discovers any preexisting health conditions, such as luxating patella or a heart murmur, you should have the right to return the puppy at the expense of the seller, who should refund the purchase price or replace the puppy with another puppy of equal value.

Remember, too, that once a breeder has accepted money or some other consideration in return for reserving a puppy, he or she has entered into an option contract. At that point the breeder cannot legally revoke or renegotiate the offer. Breeders sometimes want to do this if the puppy they have agreed to hold for a customer begins to develop into a promising-looking dog. Usually, the breeder will offer the customer another puppy. Customers do not have to take that puppy. They are within

Helpful Hints

If you give a breeder a deposit on a puppy, be sure to write "deposit for thus-and-such puppy" on the memo line of the check. Make a similar notation when you write the check for the balance of the payment. Ask for receipts for all payments made to the breeder. Find out in advance—and in writing if you wish—whether your deposit is refundable in whole or in part if you decide not to take the puppy.

their legal rights to insist upon receiving the puppy that the breeder originally agreed to sell them.

In addition to the pedigree and the sales contract, you should receive "papers" when you buy a pedigreed dog. These papers usually consist of a registration slip that you can fill out and send—along with the appropriate fee—to the administrative office of the AKC (or other relevant association) in which your puppy is eligible to be registered. In return the appropriate governing body will send you a certificate of ownership.

If you buy a dog or puppy that has been registered already by his breeder, you should receive an owner's certificate that the breeder has signed, transferring the ownership of the dog to you. Once you add your signature to that certificate of ownership, you can mail it, with the appropriate transfer fee, to the AKC, which will send you a new, amended certificate of ownership.

> **CAUTION**
>
> Read all contracts carefully before signing them. Once a contract has been signed by both parties, it becomes a legally binding document. If a contract contains any stipulations that you do not understand or do not wish to uphold, discuss these issues with the breeder before signing.

Health Certificates

Health certificates and vaccination and deworming records are the most important documents that accompany a Bulldog puppy to his new home. Do not accept a puppy without these papers. If the breeder says that he or she will send these documents "in a few days," be sure to get an extension, in writing, on the standard three to five days you normally have to get the puppy examined by a veterinarian to determine whether the puppy is healthy or whether you have legal grounds for returning him and asking for a refund.

Some breeders, especially those who produce a large number of puppies, try to save money by vaccinating their puppies themselves. There is nothing illegal about this practice, yet there is more to immunizing a puppy than drawing vaccine into a syringe and pushing the plunger. Few, if any, breeders are capable of examining puppies as thoroughly as a veterinarian can before administering vaccinations. This examination is important, because vaccine given to a sick puppy will do more harm than good. Thus, a puppy should be seen by a veterinarian at least once before that puppy is sold, preferably before his first vaccination.

Breed Needs

Although Bulldogs are justly admired for the companionship they provide us, companionship is a two-way street. In order to deserve companionship, you must be willing to provide it. If you do not enrich your Bully's life as much as he enriches yours, you are taking advantage of his good nature.

Your puppy will always be ready to lick your face when the heel marks of a frustrating day are stamped across your brow. When you are keyed up because of something the boss, the clerk at the convenience store, the person in the next cubicle at work, the president, some editorial writer, a loved one, the neighbor's kid, or some fool on the Internet did or said recently, your Bully will be happy to sit and listen to you complain about the unfairness of it all. If you are a good Bulldog owner, you will be ready to return the favor when he has had a bad day.

How to Impress a Bulldog Breeder

Expect to be asked a lot of questions by your prospective Bulldog's breeder. She will want to know, among other things, why you want a Bulldog and, more important, why a Bulldog would want you.

The best answer to the why-do-you-want-a-Bulldog question is this: "We had a wonderful, rescued Bully for six years. We had to have him put to sleep recently, and we just cannot imagine living without a Bulldog."

No one is suggesting that you claim to have owned a Bulldog when, in fact, you did not, but previous Bulldog ownership is totally the best answer to the why-do-you-want-a-Bulldog question. It is not the only answer, however, and you need not be afraid to say you have always thought Bullies were "the coolest-looking dogs."

No one denies that attractiveness is often the initial step to love, and no one is going to fault you if you were first attracted to Bulldogs because you thought they were neat looking. Many a lifelong romance of the two-legged

COMPATIBILITY Is a Bulldog the Best Breed for You?

ENERGY LEVEL	● ●
EXERCISE NEEDS	●
PERSONAL ATTENTION NEEDS	● ● ● ●
GROOMING REQUIREMENTS	● ● ●
SPACE REQUIREMENTS	● ●
AFFECTION LEVEL	● ● ● ●
PLAYFULNESS	● ● ●
FRIENDLINESS TOWARD OTHER PETS	● ● ●
FRIENDLINESS TOWARD STRANGERS	● ●
FRIENDLINESS TOWARD CHILDREN	● ● ● ●
EASE OF TRAINING	● ●
SUITABLE FOR FIRST-TIME DOG OWNERS	● ●

Grading key: 1 = least, 5 = most.

OVERVIEW: Despite his rugged good looks and robust appearance, the Bulldog is not a low-maintenance breed. Granted, his exercise needs are minimal, but his sensitivity to hot weather is a cause for concern, and his grooming requirements are significant. He is a devoted and loyal member of his pack, but he can be stubborn and single minded, too. He is a joy to be around, but that joy is tempered by the fact that his life span, roughly eight to ten years, is shorter than that of most other breeds.

variety begins because one or both parties think the other is hot, but if your affection stops at the surface, you are neither a good prospective dog owner nor a good partner.

Be Acquainted with Bulldog History

Before you inquire about a Bulldog, you should know how the breed originated and how the Bully's original purpose—the "sport" of bullbaiting—influenced his mental and physical development. In case you have not done your homework in that regard, consult "From Battlefield to Bullring," page 3. If you really want to make a good impression, arrive at the breeder's house with a dog-eared volume about Bulldogs sticking out of your bag.

Know a Bulldog's Special Needs

More important than knowing the Bulldog's history is knowing his special needs. You should be aware, for example, that a Bully is no one's first choice for long walks on the beach in the summertime. Neither is the Bully a good choice for someone who needs a "super-obedient" dog who will salute on command. Bullies are intelligent, but like many intelligent people, they are apt to trust their own intelligence as much as they do yours. Finally, you should know that Bulldogs are likely to occasion higher medical expenses than the average breed because they are prone to a number of afflictions (see Chapter 10).

Live in an Air Conditioned Place

The Bulldog is not suited for the kinds of places to which people flock to escape the winter. Indeed, the Bulldog is built for climates where people go to escape the summer. If your living space is not air conditioned—or if the rooms where your Bulldog will spend warm days are not air conditioned—your Bully will have no place where he can get comfortable. This is not fair to your Bulldog, whose breathing apparatus is the victim of fashion.

Have a Fenced-in Yard

Bulldogs may not need a lot of exercise, but they do benefit from fresh air, a change of scenery, and a chance to loaf about off leash when they are in the mood. Some people think nothing of tying their dogs out in the yard, but you should think twice before doing so. Bulldogs are not lawn ornaments. If they are going to be left outdoors, weather permitting, they should be able to move about freely. They also should have access to cool shade and fresh water.

CAUTION

Bulldogs can inspire a sense of responsibility in children, but children should never be forced to take care of dogs. Parents should remember also that when they buy puppies for their youngsters, they are buying those puppies for themselves. Inevitably even the most dog-responsible youngsters grow up and leave home, and they do not always take their dogs with them, especially when they go off to college.

Taking care of the family dog provides many people with their first taste of what it is like to be responsible for another living being. This responsibility can do wonders for a child's self-image and can help to instill a lifelong virtue of empathy, but these lessons should be learned in collaboration with—not at the expense of—a Bulldog.

Chapter Four

Caring for a Bulldog Puppy

ringing a new Bulldog puppy home is not a spur-of-the-moment affair, like deciding to have some friends over to watch a movie. You cannot simply gather up all the mess that has accumulated since the last time people came by and stuff it into the laundry room, then dash to the convenience store for a 3-pound bag of Doritos and a pint of chipotle dip.

The puppy's arrival is more like the dinner you fixed the first time your partner's mother and father came by to check you out: an event that requires forethought, afterthought, and a lot of thought in between. You have to plan the menu, do some serious shopping, place the knickknacks to best advantage, and really put on the dog.

Puppy-Proofing Your Space

Before you put out the Bulldog welcome mat, spend some time puppy-proofing your house or apartment. This inspection is best accomplished on all fours, so put yourself in your Bulldog's paws. Assume the hands-and-knees position and crawl about looking for accidents that you could make happen—a dangling tablecloth, that fancy, wrought-iron magazine rack, a jumble of dust-covered computer wires, a low-lying coffee table filled with knickknacks: If you can see it, your Bully *will* get into it. You can take that to the ATM.

Your main goal in puppy-proofing your space is to make sure your Bully cannot reach any objects you do not want him chewing or destroying. You can achieve this goal in fell swoops by closing—and dead-bolting—the doors to any rooms you do not want the puppy to explore without an escort. Also, if you have sliding glass doors, mark them with dark tape so your speeding puppy does not go slamming into them.

If your puppy is inclined to chew on electrical cords—and that is a small *if*—wrap them in heavy tape or cover them with plastic wire conduit, which you can buy in an auto-supply shop. In addition, you might want to unplug any appliance that is not in use.

Electrical sockets, too, can be a surprise to your dog. Cover them with plastic, plug-in socket guards, which you can buy at the hardware store.

CHECKLIST

The Bulldog Puppy's Wish List

✔ **Food and water bowls:** Metal or ceramic are the choice. Plastic or rubber bowls can retain odors and may set off skin allergies around your Bully's mouth and chin. Ceramic bowls should not contain lead, which can be poisonous to dogs. Bowls must be sturdy so that your Bully cannot tip them easily, and heavy enough not to break.

✔ **Rubber guards:** Stick some on the bottom of your Bully's food and water bowls so that he does not push them six ways to Sunday during an eating or drinking rapture.

✔ **Collar:** Leather or nylon, with buckle or snap. Most leather collars have belt-buckle fasteners; most nylon collars have the plastic, click-together kind. Nylon web collars with click-together fasteners are the choice for a young Bulldog puppy. They are inexpensive to replace when outgrown and easier and faster to put on and remove. When ready for a permanent collar, switch to a buckle style in either nylon or leather.

✔ **Harness:** Preferred by many owners because it does not put pressure on a dog's windpipe if he lunges forward, and there is no danger of his slipping out of it.

✔ **Leash:** Made of leather, cotton, or nylon, and may be fixed length or retractable. A retractable leash allows you to keep your Bulldog nearby when necessary or permit him to roam more freely.

✔ **Toys:** Before buying any toy for your Bulldog, imagine how it might cause him harm. If there is a chance that it could, don't buy it. Avoid any toy with a bell or whistle on the inside or a button or cute little tail on the outside.

✔ **Crate:** Whether you choose a heavy-duty plastic travel kennel or a wire crate with removable floor pan, you should put your Bully in his crate whenever he cannot be with you—at least until he is housetrained. The crate should be small enough so that he will feel cozy, but large enough to accommodate him when full grown.

✔ **Food:** Feed your Bully a premium, all-natural, holistic food, preferably made with organic, human-grade ingredients. The first ingredient should be meat; the second and third, meat or meat meal. Grains can be a source of energy for dogs, but they also can be used as filler to boost protein percentage. Any grain should be in whole form so that it supplies more fiber, vitamins, and minerals—and grains should compose no more than 10 percent of your dog's diet.

✔ **Grooming tools:** To keep your Bulldog well-groomed you will need, a brush, comb, de-shedding tool, nail clipper, styptic powder, cotton swabs, shampoo, and a tick-removal tool.

✔ **Dog beds:** Provide insulation, support, a sense of security, and a means of containing all the shed hair. They are available in many sizes, colors, materials, and designs. Whatever its construction and design, a dog bed should have a removable, washable cover.

✔ **Baby gate:** After your Bulldog has been housetrained, there may be times when you will want to confine him to a separate room. A sturdy, hinged, swing-open baby gate is essential for those times.

Next secure all low-level kitchen and bathroom cabinets with childproof locks. Make sure the lids on all trash receptacles are closed tightly. The contents of trash containers with swing-open lids could be dislodged if your Bulldog overturns the containers. If those lids cannot be secured, get new containers.

If you—or someone you love—sew, keep sewing supplies and yarn out of reach. Gather up all rubber bands, cigarettes, plastic bags, pens, pencils, or pieces of string within puppy's reach and shut them away.

If you have a fringed rug, roll it up and lock it in a spare room until your puppy emerges from the teething stage, about the age of six months. Puppy will find his way to that fringe otherwise, and you might need the services of a veterinary surgeon to find her way to the fringe trapped in puppy's intestines.

Puppy-proofing may begin at home, but it should also include the yard. Trim all low-lying branches lest puppy get a stick in the eye. Put plastic socket guards in any exposed outdoor electrical sockets, too. Make sure the fence is a tight enough fit to prevent puppy from slipping under it. If you have a swimming pool or a koi pond, it should be fenced, unless you want your Bully swimming with the fishes. Actually, the fishes would be swimming and your Bulldog . . . well, most Bullies cannot swim.

Helpful Hints

Bulldog puppies think that chair rungs are teething devices. If you do not like the look of distressed wood, move the chair(s) to the safe room where you have temporarily stashed your valuables, or wrap all exposed chair rungs in heavy tape or plastic wire conduit.

Finally, no matter how thoroughly you think you have puppy-proofed your house, your little house inspector is going to find holes in your defense. Did you overlook the mesh grill on your stereo system's sub-woofer? Puppy will pry it off one day, chew a few holes in it, and, perhaps, poke a chubby little foot through one of its cones. That is part of the price you pay for puppy's company.

Welcoming Your Puppy

After you have toted home your puppy supplies, set up a crate, deployed a dog bed or two around your house or apartment, and taken one last trouble-shooting walk around the place, it is time to bring your puppy home. If you work during the week and your employer does not provide new-puppy leave, bring puppy home at the start of a weekend or a holiday.

Keep in mind that even though you have planned carefully for this day, it will come as a large surprise to your puppy. You are taking him from a home to which he has become adjusted—and, perhaps, from the only family and friends he has ever known—and carrying him to a new land where he does not know the inhabitants, much less the customs. Being the good sort that he is, he most likely will finesse the entire operation, bouncing around his new quarters with great excitement and curiosity, pleased to be the center of attention.

Some puppies may not make the change so happily. Do not be surprised or disappointed if at first your new Bully looks more shady than a fugitive boarding a plane to a country from which he cannot be extradited. To make

BE PREPARED! Puppy Travel

If the journey from your puppy's old home to his new one is short—less than an hour's drive—and if you have a designated puppy holder along for the ride—all you will need by way of supplies are a terry cloth towel or two, a roll of paper towels, a spray bottle filled with water or a mild cleansing solution, and a plastic trash bag. For longer trips you may want to chauffeur your puppy in his crate or a small carrying kennel.

If you buy your puppy from a breeder, he or she ought to know not to feed the puppy immediately before he travels. If you plan to acquire a puppy elsewhere, find out what the feeding schedule is in that establishment and time your visit accordingly.

him feel as comfortable as possible, keep the welcoming party to a minimum. After puppy has taken the measure of his new surroundings, he will become more at ease, but that process should be taken one day, one room, and one or two family members at a time.

Actually, before you bring your new puppy *into* the house, show him the yard or the area in which he will "go outside." Hang around a bit to see if he has to go. If he does, praise him like he just got into Harvard and take him inside. If he does not have to go, Harvard can wait. Take him inside.

The room to which you introduce puppy first should be the room where he will spend most of his time—the family room or kitchen, perhaps. Make sure there is water available and a toy or two on hand for his amusement.

Unless that room has one of those fancy Dutch doors, equip it with a baby gate that is high enough to keep Bully in and low enough for you to step over without straining yourself. You could simply close the door to that room, but a baby gate allows you to peek in on Bully while he is sleeping without running the risk of violating the adage about letting sleeping dogs lie.

When bedtime arrives, your Bulldog is likely to discover for the first time in his life the true meaning of loneliness. He will feel more comfortable in his new home if he has something from his former home on hand: a familiar toy, a blanket, or a bed. These items give off familiar, comforting smells that are reassuring in a strange, new world. Moreover, nighttime will be less traumatic if you put your Bully's crate in your bedroom for a few nights until he gets used to the idea of sleeping in it.

Alternatively, you or a family member may decide to crash on the couch in the family room for the time being so the puppy does not get lonely. If you are planning to allow your Bulldog to share your bed eventually, he will be happy to settle down on the couch with you. This arrangement has the added convenience of having you close at hand when puppy has to go out at 2:00 A.M.—and the further convenience of quickening the bond between you and puppy.

The Secret of Housetraining

Although housetraining a dog is not rocket science, the term is misleading because it is you, not your dog, who needs training. As soon as you understand this, you will be ready to master the first—and only—principle of housetraining: Your dog will be housetrained as soon as you know he has to relieve himself before he does. Fortunately, this is almost as easy as it sounds. If you understand a puppy's behavior patterns, he can be housetrained with minimum difficulty and the least amount of floor cleaning.

If your Bulldog is not housetrained when you get him, you will have to take him outside many times a day. The parade begins immediately after puppy wakes up in the morning. Make sure he has at least urinated before you take him in for breakfast, and be sure to praise him generously for his achievement. Also make sure that you have taken care of any similar needs of your own beforehand in case puppy decides to explore the yard for five long, uncomfortable minutes before he gets busy.

Be aware also that some puppies are two-stage urinators. They will spend half a penny near the juniper and, after a few minutes' deliberation,

Breed Needs

Because a puppy's ability to control urination and defecation is limited, you should not acquire a Bulldog puppy who is younger than four months old if no one will be available to take him outside during the day.

HOME BASICS
The Crate: Your Other Best Friend

When your puppy has gotten acquainted with his new family, it is time for him to get acquainted with his crate. Take him outside to his toilet area first, bring him indoors, give him a minute or so to get settled, then place him in his crate with a toy. You might also help to establish your Bulldog's attachment to the crate by giving him a snack or a meal in it. Leave the crate door open and stay in the room. In a perfect world, he will begin gnawing on the toy or snack, and you will take him out of the crate in a few minutes.

Your Bully may decide, however, to quit the crate, with or without his toy. How was he supposed to know you meant for him to stay in there? Do not scold him if he beats feet. Retrieve him and the toy after a minute, then proceed to step two: putting Bully into the crate and closing the door. Remain in the room, watching television or reading or text messaging a friend. In a near-perfect world Bully will settle down with his toy.

If your Bully tries to dig his way out of the crate and/or sets up a howl, ignore him. Leave the room if you want. He is not going anywhere. When he has been quiet for at least 30 seconds, return and take him out of the crate as if nothing has happened. If you take him out of the crate while he is still in full cry, he will conclude that barking is the key that unlocks his crate.

Before long your Bulldog will be used to the idea of staying in his crate with the door closed. After he is, begin increasing the length of time he spends in the crate. He will learn to be relaxed about your comings and goings if you treat them matter-of-factly yourself, starting with the crate-training process, so do not make a big fuss—or any fuss at all—when you leave the room and he is behind bars.

By teaching your Bulldog to stay in his crate for progressively longer periods, you are preparing him to use the crate as his bed and safe haven, his own private wolf den. A dog will not soil his bed unless he is nervous or desperately needs to eliminate. Thus, if your Bulldog develops positive associations with his crate, you will be able to use it as an aid to housetraining, and he will have a secure, comfortable place to stay when you cannot supervise him.

Finally, do not hesitate to use the crate for a time-out when puppy or you need one. If, for example, puppy tries to untie your shoes while you are in them—and you have given him appropriate chew toys but he still persists in attacking your shoes—pick him up without scolding him, then deposit him and one of those appropriate toys in his crate.

the other half by the Leyland cypress. So do not scoop your boy up and whisk him inside as soon as he goes the first time. Give him a few extra minutes to await further inspiration.

In addition to his first-thing-in-the-morning walk, your Bulldog will need to go outside no more than five minutes after each meal, immediately after waking up from naps, after play sessions, just about any time he has been awake for an hour or so since the last time he was outside, and whenever he begins sniffing the floor and pacing about in a preoccupied manner. Finally, he ought to be taken outside the last thing before going to bed for the night and—because puppies cannot defer elimination for more than a few hours— at some point during the night until he is roughly four months old.

At first you will have to carry your puppy outside. As he gets older and better able to control himself, you can teach him to follow you to the door. Be sure to have a pocketful of treats—a puppy's personal GPS—when you begin this important phase of his training.

Your puppy may not urinate and defecate every time he goes out, but he ought to do one or the other on each trip if you give him enough time. Do not take him back inside no matter how cold, wet, or uncomfortable you are until you have given him 10 minutes to gather his thoughts. If he does draw a blank, put him in his crate with a toy when you get him back in the house, then try again in 15 to 20 minutes.

As your puppy matures, he will need to go outside less frequently. After he is six months old, he will be eating twice a day instead of three times, so that is one trip fewer, and he may not have to go out right after meals if he has gone out just before eating. You also will be able to dispense with the 2:00 A.M. run. Nevertheless, you will have to take your dog outside at least four times a day, 365 days a year, all the years of his life. If you find that routine inconvenient, get a cat.

When your Bulldog has an accident, do not make a federal case out of it, especially if the accident has occurred already. A puppy's attention span is no longer than a gnat's—roughly five seconds. If you leave your puppy in the kitchen after taking him outside, then walk down to get the mail, and you find a puddle on the floor when you return, do not begin screaming at the puppy. He will just as soon think you are angry because you got too many bills in the post as he will connect your outrage with his part in making that puddle. If he does begin to make a mistake in your presence, just say "No" in a loud voice, pick him up, and, holding him at a discreet distance, take him outside.

Puppy Socialization Strategies

Given their reputations as hail-fellows-well-met, an unsocialized Bulldog puppy would appear to be a contradiction in terms, but well-adjusted puppies are made, not born. Little Bullies that are not socialized properly might just as well have been raised in a cave for all the chance they have of developing into confident, well-mannered adults.

From their eighth through their sixteenth weeks, puppies mature rapidly and develop the temperament, character, and habits—good and bad—they will exhibit throughout their lives. They also work out how they will relate to their new pack, to four-legged and two-legged strangers, and to the world at large. If puppies are not handled frequently and exposed to new stimuli and experiences during this critical socialization period, the results are not

pretty. Worse yet, you will spend far more time correcting "bad" habits than you will promoting good ones.

Because you will not acquire your puppy until he is roughly 10 weeks old, you and he will be dependent on the kindness of strangers for his early socialization. Still, you will have at least six weeks in which to point the puppy's cloven little hooves on the path to model citizenship.

To borrow a sports cliché, puppy socialization consists of putting your puppy in situations where he can succeed. Toward that end . . .

Breed Truths

Socializing a Bulldog puppy plays an even greater role in his behavioral development than does his DNA.

Crank on the Sounds
Leave a radio or television playing in puppy's room to introduce him to new sounds—anything but elevator music. Run the vacuum cleaner in a distant room one day, then gradually, on subsequent days, in nearby rooms before taking it into his room. Take him into the kitchen when you use the coffee grinder or the food processor. Leave the window in his room open when you—or your landscaper—are mowing the lawn.

Expand Your Puppy's Consciousness
Rearrange some of the objects in his world: Turn a kitchen chair upside down, lay an empty wastepaper basket on its side, invert an ottoman, spray-paint a rocking chair bright green. Be creative. The floor's the limit.

Helpful Hints

Provide Self-Socialization Opportunities

Allow puppy to explore different areas of the house that he does not visit ordinarily. These field trips should be supervised and should not last long enough to challenge puppy's bladder control or any valuable objects in those rooms.

Stairway to Heaven

Make your puppy a stair master. Do so gradually, carefully, in both directions, with the aid of treats. You do not want to be toting a 65-pound (29-kg), stairphobic, adult Bulldog to visit your aunt Millie in her third-floor walkup.

Be Touchy-Feely

Sell your puppy on the idea that you are allowed to touch him whenever, wherever you please. While holding him on your lap telling him he is the greatest thing since take-out food, hold his feet, rub his face, run your finger over his teeth, fiddle with his ears, whatever. If he objects, growl *"Nah!"* or *"Quit!"* or both in your do-not-tick-me-off voice. When he quits, praise him warmly, then continue to let your fingers do the walking. You will thank yourself when it is time to brush him, bathe him, clean his ears, dredge the wrinkles on his face, or, especially, clip his nails.

Host Puppy-Warming Parties

Invite one or two people over to meet your new guy. Aim for diversity: Invite men, women, young folks, old folks, yuppies, cross-dressers, beards, longhairs, no-hairs, and people from different ethnic backgrounds. The more people he meets, the merrier the puppy will grow up to be.

Rent a Pet

If you do not have other animals, invite a friendly, healthy, vaccinated dog or puppy that belongs to one of your friends over to meet your guy for play, mutual butt sniffing, and long afternoons in front of the fireplace.

FYI: Antigens and Antibodies

When the antigens contained in a vaccine begin circulating in your Bully's bloodstream, they are detected and seized upon by specialized cells that are part of his body's immune system. After a series of complex evolutions, the immune system produces cells that are able to detect and destroy the diseases represented by the antigens contained in a vaccine. Thus, if a Bulldog vaccinated against distemper was later exposed to the virus, distemper antibodies would recognize and exterminate any free-ranging distemper virus particles at large in his bloodstream. Even if the distemper invaders managed to infect some of the Bully's cells, those infected cells would be recognized, destroyed, and shown the door by other specialized cells in the immune system.

Go for a Ride

Take your puppy for brief car rides. Enlist a friend or family member to hold puppy in case you decide to stop at Starbucks for a latte. Hit McDonald's drive-through window. The sales associate there should be good for a dog biscuit.

Stroll the Boulevard

Introduce your puppy to outdoor cafés, flea markets, parks, playgrounds, demonstrations, tailgate parties, the nearest big-box pet store—anyplace he is likely to meet new people. The puppy who has never met a stranger has, in reality, met lots of strangers whom he has turned into friends.

Vaccinations

Science tells us that until puppies are roughly six to eight weeks of age, they are protected from certain diseases by antibodies in their mothers' milk, as long as their mothers have been immunized properly against those diseases and possess the antibodies needed to pass on that immunity. Because this passive immunity can interfere with puppies' ability to produce their own antibodies in response to being vaccinated, many veterinarians recommend that puppies not be vaccinated for the first time until they are at least six weeks old.

Some veterinarians put that starting age at eight weeks. Indeed, there are nearly as many opinions about vaccination and booster-shot schedules as there are recipes for making chili. The important thing is to find a competent veterinarian and to do what he or she tells you.

The vaccine given to puppies contains antigens that have been derived ultimately from viruses or bacteria obtained from live animals. Typically, a

puppy is vaccinated against some or all of the following conditions: distemper, an airborne viral disease that affects the lungs, intestines and brain; hepatitis, a viral disease of the liver; leptospirosis, a bacterial disease that attacks the urinary system; parainfluenza (infectious bronchitis); parvovirus, a viral disease of the intestines; corona viruses, which attack the intestines; bordetella (kennel cough); and Lyme disease.

One vaccination does not confer instant immunity on a puppy. Not for five to ten days will his immune system start to forge a response to the challenge posed by the antigens in a vaccine. That response is low grade and not entirely effective. What is more,

CAUTION

Until your puppy has been vaccinated fully, about the age of four months, do not allow him to walk where unknown—and possibly sick—animals may have walked. Wait until a week after your puppy has received his final vaccination before allowing him to walk a mile in other dogs' paw prints.

BE PREPARED! Sample Puppy Vaccination Schedule

Puppy's Age	Type of Vaccine Administered
5 Weeks*	Parvovirus—administered only if a puppy is considered to be at high risk for infection.
6 Weeks*	Five-way combination vaccine that includes adenovirus cough, hepatitis, canine distemper, parainfluenza, and parvovirus. Some combination vaccines may also include leptospirosis and/or corona virus if those diseases are prevalent in the area where the puppy resides. Ask your veterinarian for guidance in this regard, as not all veterinarians recommend corona virus vaccine.
9 Weeks**	Same as above. (Note: the inclusion of either canine adenovirus-1 or adenovirus-2 in a vaccine protects against adenovirus cough and hepatitis; adenovirus-2 is preferred by most veterinarians.)
12 Weeks	Same as above. Add Lyme vaccine if Lyme disease is prevalent in puppy's locale or in an area to which puppy will be traveling.
12 Weeks or Older	Rabies vaccination as required by local ordinance.
15 Weeks	Once again a five- or seven-way vaccine.

*Should have been administered by a veterinarian at your puppy's breeder's request. Ask for vaccination certificate signed and dated by the administering veterinarian.

** If you purchased a puppy older than nine weeks of age, this vaccination also should have been administered already. As before, ask for a signed and dated vaccination certificate.

you can never be certain how long a puppy's passive immunity will continue to compromise his ability to manufacture his own antibodies. For these reasons all veterinarians revaccinate a puppy in two, three, or four weeks, and many veterinarians re-revaccinate four weeks after the second vaccination, if not sooner. After that, dogs should receive booster shots every year—or every two to three years, according to some veterinarians—because antibodies decrease in number over time and the immune system needs to be re-stimulated to produce additional disease-fighting troops.

The initial rabies vaccination is administered to dogs when they are three months old. Most veterinarians boost that shot when a dog is a year old and then boost it every year or two thereafter.

As the fine print at the bottom of football pools informs us, the preceding material is intended for educational purposes only. It is not intended to take the place of qualified veterinary consultation.

Chapter Five

Living with
a Bulldog

N o matter what your family configuration, when a Bulldog enters that family, it becomes a pack—even if it is only a pack of two—and as far as the Bulldog is concerned, somebody has to assume leadership of that pack. If your little sour-mug had been born into a Bulldog pack in the wild—an amusing notion, but let us accept it nevertheless for purposes of illustration—he would know his place in that pack before long, a place pretty much at the bottom of the pecking order. That would be fine with him. Those wild, free-ranging Bulldogs derive their sense of security from knowing what their place is, not, as humans often do, from basking in the importance of that place.

Qualities of a Good Pack Leader

The best human pack leaders are the ones who can put themselves in a dog's place. Some people are born with this ability, some are not, but good pack leaders can be made as well as born. To see if you qualify as a good pack leader, ask yourself this: Would I think I was a good pack leader if I was my Bulldog?

This is the deal breaker, yet few people think to ask themselves if they would make good pack leaders. They might spend time "researching" Bulldogs and worrying if Bullies shed, if they bark a lot, if they require much in the way of care and maintenance, and so forth, but they never get around to asking themselves if they have the right stuff to be a good pack leader.

Our Bullies will consider us good pack leaders if we . . .

- do not scold them for doing something today that we thought was cute yesterday.
- do not correct them for something they did ten minutes ago—or even two minutes ago—that they have long forgotten by the time we correct them.
- remain calm, assertive, and in control when we correct them.
- remember that the best time to correct a dog is when he is about to do something "wrong," not when he is fully engaged in that activity.
- praise them when they have done something praiseworthy.

FYI: The Alpha-Dog Principle

Dogs have always depended on the ability to function within a social hierarchy to survive, a dependence that leads them to seek our approval. In the wild, dogs and their wolfish relatives live in a hierarchy dominated by the alpha member, or leader, of the pack. The alpha dog, who is generally a female, is judge, jury, sheriff, exalted ruler, and high priestess of the pack. When the alpha dog wants to rest, the other members of the pack lie down. When the alpha dog wants to move on, the pack follows. When the alpha dog wants to hunt, the pack members sharpen their fangs.

This centuries-old predisposition to function in a follow-the-leader arrangement makes it possible for us to assume the role of alpha dog in our Bullies' lives. This principle also makes it possible for dogs to dominate people who are bigger—and sometimes more intelligent—than their four-legged tyrants.

Just as nature abhors a vacuum, pack animals abhor a democracy. Every pack must have a leader. If you do not want the job, your Bulldog will take it. Before you allow this to happen, remember that if you are not the lead dog In the pack, the scenery seldom changes.

The Name Game

After you have chosen a name for your Bulldog—something manly yet whimsical like "Bronco," for example—begin teaching him that name by building positive associations with it. Say *"Bronco"* before you pet him, before you put his food bowl down for him, and before you take him outside to play. Soon *"Bronco"* will be music to his ears.

You can make that music sweeter by rewarding Bronco for responding to it. While you are playing with him or just hanging out together, say *"Bronco"* with great enthusiasm. If he looks in any direction but yours, count to three and say his name again. Bronco will look toward you eventually. When he does, say *"Good boy"* and give him a treat.

Now that you have Bronco's attention, wait a minute or so until he turns his attention elsewhere, then say his name once more. You may have to say it two or three times, but if you put enough excitement into your voice—

Breed Needs

Quite often a Bulldog's name and a feeling of confusion are the only things he brings with him to his new home. If your Bully already has a name and he knows what it is, why not let him keep it? You may shorten it some, if possible, or reshape it to your liking, but your Bulldog has enough to do adjusting to a new home without having to adjust to a new identity as well.

and a tempting treat in your hand—Bronco will look at you again. When he does, make a fuss over him as you did before and give him a treat.

After Bronco has responded to his name three or four times in one session, you have accomplished your mission. If you repeat that mission two or three times a day for several days, you will have Bronco's attention anytime you say his name.

A Bulldog often has more than one name. If he is registered with the American Kennel Club or another breed registry, he has the "official" name by which he was registered—Bullfeather's Pomp and Circumstance, for example. Because standing on the back porch yelling, "Here, Pomp and Circumstance" can get your trees toilet-papered in some neighborhoods, many Bulldog owners give their dogs what are known as "call names," terms of endearment by which the dogs are known to their families and friends. Pomp and Circumstance easily lends itself to Pom-Pom, Stomper, Circus, and other nicknames. Sometimes a call name has nothing to do with an official name, which is how Pomp and Circumstance might just end up being called Booger.

Bulldogs and Children and Other Pets

Children and puppies are two of this culture's favorite photo opportunities. In real life, however, negotiations between the two are not always picture perfect. Children who are too young or immature to "play nice with puppy" can threaten his sense of confidence and make him hand shy or even worse.

Before a child can be allowed unsupervised interactions with a puppy, the child must be mature enough to understand that puppies—even Bulldog puppies, who are hardwired to get along with children—do not like to be disturbed when they are eating or sleeping. Children must understand also

BE PREPARED! Mutiny of the Bully

In addition to asking yourself if you have the makings of a good pack leader, ask yourself if your Bulldog's behavior indicates that he has designs on your job.

- Does he stand in front of you and bark when he wants something?
- Does he jump up on you whenever he feels like it?
- Does he paw at you or drop toys into your lap when he wants to play?
- Does he snatch your food and run away with it?
- Does he play keep-away with your possessions?
- Does he give you a look that says "can't catch me" when you call him?
- Is he insistent and unreasonable?

that there is a correct way to hold a puppy, that puppy's ears and tail are not handles, and that they (children) should never run with a puppy in their arms as though he were a football. The age at which these lessons can be learned varies from one child to the next, but as a rule, parents should wait to get a puppy until their children are roughly four years old.

Even if parents think their children can be trusted to play with a Bulldog puppy without mugging him, they should explain that what is fun for children may not be fun for a puppy. They also should explain that children must be careful where they walk and run when puppy is around—and that puppies often are frightened by loud, unfamiliar sounds.

Caution children to speak and play quietly until the puppy gets used to them. Tell them not to pick the puppy up until you feel he is comfortable enough not to be frightened by a sudden ride. Teach children the proper way to hold a puppy: one hand under his rib cage just behind his front legs, the other hand under his bottom, with puppy's face pointing away from theirs. Have them practice this while sitting down in case they drop the puppy or he jumps from their arms.

Bulldogs and Other Pets

If you have other pets, manage the introductions between them and your Bulldog carefully. Do not include them in the welcoming party when you bring your new Bulldog puppy home. Confine your cat to another part of the house or apartment from which she cannot escape. Do the same with your dog(s).

Indeed you do not have to introduce your puppy to your other animals on puppy's first day home, especially if he had a two-hour car ride from his former residence. Tomorrow or the next day is soon enough to make introductions.

If you have more than one other dog, introduce them to puppy one at a time, but not one right after the other. Put puppy into his crate before letting the older dog into the room. If the older dog sniffs at the puppy in curiosity but shows no hostility—raised hackles, flattened ears, growling, or lifting his leg on the crate—put a leash on the older dog and let the puppy out of his crate. The less tension there is between the two dogs, the less tension you will feel on the leash.

If your older dog crouches ominously, tug on the leash quickly and with enough authority to keep him from reaching the puppy. Then lead the older dog out of the room and try the introduction again the following day. If the introduction goes well, give each dog a treat, the older dog first, of course, to reinforce civil behavior.

Before letting your cat in to see the puppy, be sure her claws are clipped. Put the puppy in his crate, then give the two animals time to sniff at each other. If your cat is leash trained, put a leash on her when you bring her in to meet the puppy. If not, stay close to her and the puppy. Chances are, a puppy-cat introduction will not go as smoothly as a puppy-dog introduction, but this does not mean that your puppy and your cat will not be able to coexist peacefully.

The chances of hostilities breaking out between your new Bulldog and your present pets vary inversely with the ages of your other pets and the length of time you have owned them. If you have an eight-year-old only pet, he may not respond cheerfully to a new puppy. If your pet is four years old or younger, you should be able to introduce a new Bulldog if you manage the introduction smartly—and if you consider how you would feel if a stranger was brought to your house suddenly for an indefinite stay without your prior approval.

Helpful Hints

Do not use your Bulldog's name when you need to scold him. If he is chasing the cat or using one of your shoes for a chew toy, clap your hands together sharply and holler, *"No!"* Leave his name out of this equation.

Introducing the Collar or Harness

After your new Bully has had time to get comfortable with you and his new living space, give him a chance to get comfortable with a collar. This is a two-step process: Put the collar around his neck; see what happens next.

The stealth method of introducing a collar consists of putting it around your Bully's neck just before you feed him. Bullies are such eager eaters that you could drape 3 pounds (1.5 kg) of bling on a chain around their necks before feeding them, and they would not notice.

Remove the collar after puppy has eaten, before you take him outside for his post-meal walk. After a few days, put the collar on him at other times during the day, leaving the collar on a little longer each time. In about a week add his identification and license tags to the collar.

Introducing a harness to your Bulldog is hardly more complicated than introducing a collar. After spending a few moments playing with or petting your Bulldog, set the harness on his back but do not buckle it. If he appears uncomfortable—i.e., if he rolls madly on the floor, scratches at the harness,

or appears to go into a catatonic state—talk reassuringly to him, pet him a few seconds, remove the harness, and try again the next day. If he does not seem to mind the harness, hook it up and be done with it.

Be sure to give your Bully a treat once the harness is in place. Do not give him a treat if he recoils from the harness.

After your Bulldog has accepted the harness, leave it on for five or ten minutes a day for several days. Then leave it on for 10 or 15 minutes a day and, finally, for 15 to 20 minutes a day after that.

Why You Should Alter Your Bulldog

Altered dogs make better companions because they are more civilized than dogs that are sexually intact. Unaltered males, for example, will lift their legs to squirt the refrigerator or the lounge chair with urine as a means of marking territory and attracting females—even if there are no Bulldog females in the house. Now, *that* is optimism. Unaltered males also are inclined to make sexual advances at people's legs and to regard any other dog as either a potential mate or a sparring partner.

Most unaltered females come into season (or heat) twice a year. The indications of this condition are vulvar swelling, blood spots that will need to be removed from the rug(s), and, quite frequently, unannounced visits from neighborhood dogs who loiter around the yard peeing all over everything. The average heat lasts 21 days, but those 21 days will seem longer than the three weeks before Christmas did when you were a child.

Bulldogs should be altered at an age when their sexual development is nearly complete, but undesirable traits—urine marking by male dogs, for example—have not become habits. Most veterinarians suggest that this age occurs for females when they are about six months old. Males should be neutered when they are seven to ten months old.

In addition, there are socially redeeming reasons for altering your Bulldog. Too many puppies are produced for no better reason than letting children observe the "miracle" of birth. Such misguided parents should let their children watch one of their own species being born—or take Jason and Sis to an animal shelter and let them witness the downside of the miracle of birth: the euthanasia of homeless dogs, who invariably go to meet the needle with their tails wagging.

Neither spaying or neutering is burdensome on a healthy young Bulldog. Spaying is somewhat more complicated and, therefore takes longer than neutering does, because females wear their reproductive organs on the inside. Neutering is a snap, comparatively, because testicles are external to their owners.

Veterinarians generally want to keep overnight a dog that has been neutered or spayed to make sure that he or she recovers fully from the anesthetic. Roughly 10 days after the operation, you will take your Bully back to the veterinarian to have the stitches removed.

Coping with Separation Anxiety

The causes of separation anxiety are not understood completely. Some dogs suffer from it and, under similar circumstances, others do not. What we do know is that separation anxiety can occur when a dog that has rarely or never been left alone finds himself in an empty house; when a dog is left home alone after a period, such as a vacation or illness, when he and his owner were together constantly; after an unhappy stay in a boarding kennel; or because of an upheaval in the daily routine—a child who had been the dog's best friend goes off to college or an adult who had been telecommuting starts working outside of the home full time.

The symptoms of separation anxiety resemble those of your basic cyclone. As dogs become anxious, then more anxious, then frantic when their owners leave home without them, they may whine or howl or bark nonstop. They may drool, pant, lick themselves, chew themselves, or vomit. They may destroy whatever they can get their teeth and paws on, and relieve themselves in an effort to relieve their anxiety. They even may try a jailbreak—digging, chewing, and scratching at doors or windows, or even trying to jump, through a window—in an attempt to escape and reunite with their owners.

When separation anxiety is minor—that is, when your dog does not try to tunnel out of the house in your absence—the following strategies may alleviate the problem.

- Do not make a big deal out of arrivals or departures. Leave the house without fawning over your dog to reassure him that you will be right back.
- Do not greet him as though you have been away for six months when you have merely been grocery shopping.
- Leave your dog something to remember you by when you are away. Give him the shirt off your back or the pillowcase off your bed.
- Act as though you are getting ready to leave—fetch your keys, put on your coat—then sit back down. Do this until your dog shows no signs of being upset by these activities.

Breed Needs

The behavioral approach to treating separation anxiety requires time and patience, items that may be in short supply. If so, ask your veterinarian if he or she can prescribe medication that reduces your dog's anxiety without sedating him. This will buy you and your dog some time while you proceed with his reprogramming.

- Act as though you are getting ready to leave, but before you sit back down, go to the door, then open and close it. Repeat as necessary until your dog is not dismayed by that behavior.
- Ditto, except this time leave the door open before you return to your dog.
- The big test: Step outside, close the door, count to one, then return immediately to your dog before he has a chance to start climbing the drapes.
- Repeat this step, gradually counting to two, then three, then five until your dog is accustomed to being alone with the door closed for a short stretch.

BE PREPARED! The First-Aid Kit

Bulldogs, unfortunately, are not exempt from mishaps. Bulldog owners, therefore, must be prepared in case of emergency. This means having more in their family's canine first-aid kit than the veterinarian's phone number, a towel, and a spray bottle filled with some kind of odor-killing liquid. In addition to those items, which do have their usefulness, the first-aid kit should contain the following:

- Gauze sponges
- A roll of narrow gauze
- A roll of bandages, such as a gauze wrap that stretches and clings
- Hypoallergenic adhesive tape
- Non-adherent sterile pads
- Absorbent cotton
- A water-based sterile lubricant
- 3 percent hydrogen peroxide
- Rubbing alcohol
- A topical antibiotic ointment
- Hydrocortisone ointment
- Epsom salts
- A sterile eye lubricant
- A sterile saline eye wash
- Styptic powder or pencil
- Petroleum jelly
- Small scissors with rounded tips
- A pediatric rectal thermometer
- Tweezers
- An unbreakable, baby-dose syringe or eye dropper
- A 2-ounce-capacity ear syringe
- A blanket

- A muzzle
- Splints
- Your Bully's vital statistics (weight, age, medical conditions)
- A veterinary first aid manual
- The ASPCA National Animal Poison Control Center phone number: (800) 548-2423

Should emergency strike your Bulldog, do not make matters worse by getting hysterical. Do not grab him to reassure him either. You may wind up getting bitten for your trouble. If your Bully is unable to get to the veterinarian's under his own power—that is, on a leash—you will need to use a stretcher if you have one, or else you'll need to fashion one from a sheet or blanket. If you think it is necessary, put a muzzle on your dog. If you do not own a muzzle, you can try to fashion one out of a strip of gauze or a large towel, but this is easier said than done with a short-muzzled breed.

If your Bulldog is unconscious, observe his chest or flank for signs of breathing, or hold a wet finger in front of his nostrils. Make sure that nothing is obstructing his breathing, then look for signs of bleeding. Arterial bleeding is bright red, difficult to stop, and spurts from the wound. If your dog is bleeding, place a folded, clean cloth over the wound and apply gentle, direct pressure for five to ten minutes.

If your dog becomes anxious at any point during this process, do not soothe him. That will reinforce his anxiety. Calmly return to a point in the drill that did not make him antsy, then repeat that step for several days before proceeding.

When you think your dog is ready to be alone for more than five seconds, give him a verbal cue such as a flat *"I'll be back,"* then leave him alone for

a minute. Do not act as though he hit the lottery in your absence when you return.

If your dog shows no signs of anxiety at being left alone for a full minute, go for a minute and a half after a few days, with the goal of being able to leave him for 30 minutes or so at a time.

This might all seem tedious, but so is having to replace an article of furniture every time you return home from a trip to the mall.

Traveling with Your Bulldog

The film *Peter's Friends* features a character named Maggie, who cannot bear to be away from her cat. Before Maggie, played by Emma Thompson, prepares to go on vacation to visit friends she has not seen in ten years, she papers the walls of her house with photographs of herself so that her cat, for whom she has arranged a pet sitter, will not be lonely or—worse yet—forget her while she is gone.

If Maggie were a dog owner, she could save the wear and tear on her walls by hauling her dog with her to see her friends, for dogs are the world's most eager and willing travelers. They can detect the sub-audible rustling of car keys from any room in the house, and they read body language so keenly

69

BE PREPARED! Overnight Trips

Carry your Bulldog's medical history with you if you plan to be away from home overnight with him. Be sure to include all pertinent information in an emergency kit along with copies of health certificates and identification information.

If you can, secure the names and phone numbers of veterinarians in the area where you and your Bully will be staying. Failing that, take the American Animal Hospital Association's phone number along—(800) 883-6301.

they are able to tell by the way we walk whether we are simply going out to pick up the paper from the lawn or going somewhere in the car. In the latter case they are at the door before we are, wagging their tails, lolling their tongues, and bouncing around gleefully. Bulldogs should not begin car training until they have mastered housetraining.

Although many articles about traveling with dogs take the vertical liftoff approach and begin straightaway with advice about air travel, most dogs make their first (and only) journeys at lower altitudes. We will begin, therefore, with a few tips about ground travel with your Bulldog.

Car Sense

The first rule of car travel is this: Bulldogs should never be allowed to ride free in a car. Nine times out of ten nothing bad will befall them if they do. The tenth time you will have to slam on the brakes when some driver talking on a cell phone in another car drifts into your lane, and your Bully will become a 50-pound (23-kg) projectile whizzing toward the dashboard. The first rule of car travel is this: Bulldogs should never be allowed to ride free in a car.

CHECKLIST

Travel Essentials

- ✔ Carrier
- ✔ Food (single-meal-size, pop top cans; packets of moist food; and or resealable bags of dry food
- ✔ Bottled water
- ✔ Food and water bowls
- ✔ Spoons or forks or both
- ✔ Disposable plastic bags
- ✔ Collar and/or harness
- ✔ Leash

- ✔ Dog bed
- ✔ Medications if necessary
- ✔ Cotton balls and cotton swabs
- ✔ Brush
- ✔ Toys
- ✔ Mineral oil
- ✔ Sponge, paper towels, moistened towelettes
- ✔ Emergency first-aid kit (see page 68)

Now that you have a crate or a car seat for your Bully, put him in it and go for a short trip to the convenience store and back. This will give you an opportunity to find out if your dog is prone to motion sickness, a discovery you do not want to make 15 minutes after you have set out on a 200-mile jaunt to grandmother's house for Thanksgiving.

Position your Bully's traveling crate where it will not slide around if you have to make a sudden stop or take a sharp corner. Anchor the crate with a seat belt if possible, and keep the crate well away from airbags. Put a blanket and a soft toy in the crate, but no food or water dishes.

If your Bully is prone to motion sickness, do not give him any food or water for at least four hours before you turn the key in the ignition. If the trip lasts more than four hours, be sure to give him water and occasional rest stops about every three hours or so, more frequently if necessary.

Plan to eat at drive-through restaurants or pack some food for the trip. If time permits, pack a picnic and stop at a park or rest stop. This way, you can take your Bully for a walk on his leash, so he can stretch his legs and relieve himself.

If you are traveling in hot weather, be sure to pack ice, ice packs, and water in a cooler, in addition to packing a cooling blanket or vest for your Bully. You and he will be thankful that you did if your vehicle breaks down and you need to keep your Bully cool until help arrives. Better yet, do not make automobile trips in hot weather unless they are absolutely necessary.

Finding Accommodations

It is possible to find hotels and motels throughout the United States and Canada that will accommodate pets, but even if a facility is listed as pet-friendly, you should phone ahead for reservations and discuss their terms and conditions. Some establishments that accept pets limit the number of rooms for travelers with pets, and some places may require pets to be housed in a separate kennel facility.

If you are staying with friends or relatives, make sure your dog is welcome and can be housed comfortably. Find out if any members of the host family have canine-related allergies. If there are other pets in the host household, how will your Bulldog get along with them? Bulldogs have a reputation for getting along with other animals, but that is not always a two-way street.

Hotel Safety Tips

Hotels and motels that accept dogs often make dog owners jump through hoops in return for that privilege. In addition to charging more money for pet rooms, motels virtually make you promise in blood that you will not leave your dog(s) alone in the room unless they are crated. Fair enough, but some places demand that your dog(s) never be left alone in the room at all. That really makes sense. Do they think you have driven 1,000 miles to spend three days in a motel room watching television with your dog?

Inspect the room before bringing your dog inside, and take any necessary dog-proofing measures. Check the room for dog hiding places or places in which your Bully might become trapped. Use masking tape and heavy paper or pillows to block access to these attractive nuisances.

Ask if and when the room you have been assigned was sprayed with insecticide. If it was sprayed recently, ask for another room. You do not

CAUTION

Be sure to hang the "Do Not Disturb" sign outside your hotel or motel room door whenever you leave your Bully in the room, even if he is in his crate.

want to expose your Bully to insecticides. Also, beware of toilets with blue toilet water, which can be poisonous. To be safe, keep the toilet lid closed so your Bully cannot drink the water. Make sure all drawers, windows, and doors are closed before you let your Bully out to explore.

Pretravel Health Check

Your Bulldog's vaccinations must be up to date, and you should have proper vaccination and health certificates before you and he leave home. These are required for any kind of airline travel. They also may be necessary if your Bully gets into a fight with another animal or bites or scratches someone. Place the certificates in your emergency kit.

Although the use of tranquilizers is generally discouraged, some dogs require sedation in order to travel. If you think your Bully might benefit

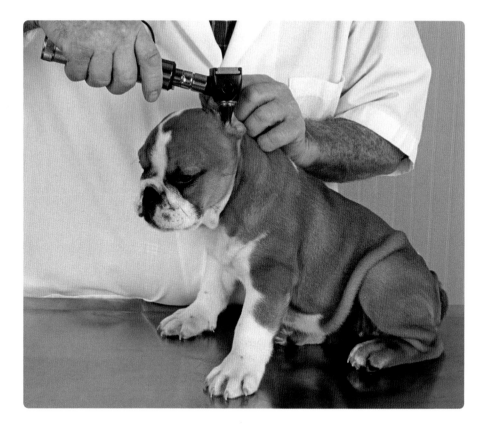

from tranquilizers, discuss their use with his veterinarian. Sedatives have been cited for contributing to death from overheating among canine airline passengers.

The Friendly Skies

Animals cannot be shipped by train or bus, but your Bulldog can catch a plane, weather permitting—that is, if the temperature does not exceed 85°F (29.4°C) or fall below 45°F (7.2°Cs) in the baggage compartment of an airplane. In general, if temperatures fall outside that range in either the departure or the destination city, animals are grounded.

The responsibility for finding out about temperature and other airline regulations is on you. While you are doing your research, consider the following: Until 2005, when the U.S. Department of Transportation began requiring airlines to file monthly reports on incidents involving pets, there was no way of knowing

Breed Truths

Airlines may impose more stringent temperature restrictions on brachycephalic (short-face) breeds such as the Bulldog, who may be denied boarding privileges when temperatures exceed 70°F (21.1°C).

how many pets were killed, injured, or lost while traveling by air.

Sixteen months after that ruling went into effect, the *Atlanta Journal-Constitution* reported that 45 pets had died as a result of flying, 23 had been injured, and 11 had been lost. As unfortunate as those incidents were, they constituted a fraction of 1 percent of the roughly 1 million companion animals estimated to fly each year.

All travel puts a strain on pets. Air travel puts more. If you want to take your Bully with you on a short

Breed Needs

Even the most reliable Bulldogs may have an accident owing to the stress of air travel. If he does, he will thank you for having thought to line the bottom of his carrier with a soft, absorbent rug or a layer of shredded newspaper under a fleece cover.

trip or a vacation, and that journey involves flying, you should ask yourself why you want to take him along. Is it because you will be happier? Or he will be happier? If you cannot truthfully say that your Bully would gladly submit to round-trip air travel to be with you—when he could be getting cheap with the pet sitter two or three times a day or hanging out at Uncle Mort's or even at a posh boarding kennel—then leave him home. He will forget the pet sitter as soon as he sees you, he will be tired of old Mort in a week anyway, and if you choose a kennel carefully, he may think he has been at a spa.

If you really believe your Bully cannot survive a week without the sound of your voice, you can always leave the volume turned up on the answering machine, call home twice a day, and sing "You Are the Sunshine of My Life" to your befuddled pal. Do not laugh. It happens.

In the Hold

Bulldogs cannot fit into a shoe-box carrier that can be stowed under a seat in an airplane's cabin, so they must travel in the cargo hold as excess baggage, not the most flattering of terms. Therefore, if you plan to ship your Bully by air, you will need a kennel that is at least big enough to allow him to stand up and turn around in while he is wondering where you have gone and why you have left him in this weird place.

The best carrier for transporting a Bulldog by air is an airline-approved model constructed of heavy-molded plastic. There must be a provision for securing a water dish to the inside of the kennel, and the dish should be installed in such a way that airline personnel can reach it if necessary without having to open the carrier.

Pets shipped as excess baggage travel with passengers' luggage in a part of the plane that is illuminated and maintained at the same pressurization and temperature as the passenger cabins. Pet kennels are kept separate from the Guccis and the Vuittons in this area, and are usually stowed near the door for quick access.

When your Bulldog travels as excess baggage, you surrender him at the ticket counter before boarding your flight. This means that he is onloaded—as they say in the airline industry—directly onto the plane from there.

Because oxygen is limited in the hold, you will need to make a reservation for your Bully. Try to get a nonstop flight. Failing that, try to find a direct flight so your Bully does not have to be taken off one plane and put onto another, thereby geometrically increasing the chances of accidental transfers or delays. Keep in mind, too, that you have to be at the airport about two hours before departure time to have your dog checked in, and you will be an extra half hour or so collecting him when you get to where you are going.

Having catalogued the problems that attend flying, we must say this: If you have no choice in the matter, or if you are determined to do it anyway because the Keys just would not be the same without ol' Bronco, flying is not an automatic death sentence. Thousands of animals do arrive at their destinations in one piece—and on the first try—every day of the year.

Paperwork and Planning

Most airlines require that traveling pets arrive with health certificates issued by a certified veterinarian within the last 10 to 30 days. Moreover, some states require that pets' vaccinations, particularly rabies shots, are current. (The veterinarian will testify somewhere on the health certificate that they are.) Even if a health certificate is not required, your Bulldog should have a preflight checkup at the veterinarian's in any case. If an aging dog has developed a heart condition since his last exam, the friendly skies might not be so friendly to his health.

CAUTION

Some airlines suggest that you tranquilize your dog before putting him on a plane, but that is not a good idea for Bulldogs, especially those with unresolved breathing difficulties that result from elongated soft palate, stenotic nares, or hypoplastic trachea. Furthermore, tranquilizers can have a paradoxical effect on animals—stimulating them instead of sedating them.

If your Bully is not used to the idea of a travel kennel, obtain one several days before your departure. Most kennels can be taken apart. Do that, and see if your Bully will use one half of the kennel for a bed if you put one of his blankets and a toy in it. Also try feeding him in the kennel. The trip will be a lot less stressful if he thinks of the kennel as a friendly device and associates it with one or the other of his preferred activities.

A favorite blanket, towel, or toy is another way to improve the atmosphere in the kennel during a flight. Make sure the toy is something soft that you can secure to the inside of the kennel. You do not want Bronco coldcocked by a flying chew bone high over Kansas.

If your Bully sleeps on or near your pillow at night, take a freshly used pillowcase and sew it around a piece of foam rubber that has been cut to fit the bottom of the cage. If you think he would like more privacy, line a portion of the inside of the kennel door with a disposable diaper—but not a Baby Huey–size diaper that cuts off air circulation. All you want to do is cover enough of the front door to create a sense of security.

Do not feed your Bully within 10 to 12 hours of flight time. The preflight meal should be a light one—a little chicken and rice, perhaps, not a two-course, kibble-and-red-meat feast. What is more, dogs should not be given too much water before a flight.

Helpful Hints

You can help your Bulldog keep his cool in flight if you fill his water dish the night before and put it in the freezer; and you can help yourself keep your cool if you attach a note to his crate reminding yourself not to forget his water dish. A water dish with a wall-to-wall ice cube in it gives your Bully the options of licking the ice or drinking the water as the ice melts. Besides, frozen water seldom spills.

The Receiving End

If you are not traveling on the same flight as your Bulldog or if you are not picking him up yourself, make sure there is someone reliable to meet him. Be sure the kennel is marked on the outside with your Bully's destination and the phone numbers where you or the person picking him up can be reached at all times. These numbers, which are critical if the flight or the person meeting the flight is delayed, should also be affixed to your Bully's collar. Instructions that specify his daily feeding and watering schedule should be attached to the kennel, too. This schedule will help airline personnel to care for your Bully in the event that he goes east while you go west.

Putting your Bully on an airplane is not like handing him over to the Grim Reaper. Most dogs survive their fear of flying, and many people who ship dogs by air report that the dogs come out of their kennels with a handshake and a wagging tail. Why not? Dogs do not have to eat airline food or watch movies they have seen already.

Whom to Call

The regulations that airlines must follow when transporting animals are issued by the United States Department of Agriculture (USDA) and the International Air Transport Association (IATA). If you have any questions that the airlines cannot answer—or if you do not understand the answers you receive from an airline—you can contact the USDA at (800) 545-8732. The number for the IATA's regional office in the United States is (202) 293-9292.

Laws, customs, and quarantine regulations vary from one country to the next, so extra care and planning is needed if you are considering an overseas jaunt with your dog. Contact the IATA and the airlines on which you are considering traveling well in advance of the day you plan to leave on your journey.

If Your Bulldog Gets Lost

Whenever your Bulldog leaves home, he should wear his collar with the appropriate tags attached in case he becomes lost. Those tags should include his name, and your name, address, and telephone number. If you have a microchip implanted in your dog, another tag should inform anyone who finds your dog that he has been microchipped for easy identification.

An emergency kit with additional information will further aid in your Bully's recovery. Assemble an envelope containing medical and vaccination records, ownership papers or other documentation such as veterinary records; the name and phone number of your Bully's veterinarian, and a current photograph of your dog.

If your Bully goes missing, contact animal control agencies and humane societies in the local and surrounding areas. Provide descriptions and photographs and check with them daily. Contact the Animal and Plant Health Inspection Service Animal Care regional office closest to where your Bully was lost. Seek help from local radio and television stations. Use the current photograph of your Bully that you packed in his emergency kit to make lost-Bulldog fliers to post all over the area in which he was lost. Leave telephone numbers and addresses with the various people and agencies you have contacted if you have to return home before your Bully has been found.

Chapter Six

Bulldog Health and Nutrition

When Bulldogs are ailing, they cannot tell us in so many words where it hurts. Their behavior *can* tell us that something is not right, and it is our job to relay that message to a veterinarian. A lack of appetite is often the first suggestion that a Bulldog is not well. If your Bully skips a meal or sniffs at his bowl as though he would send it back to the chef if he could, there may be cause for concern even if he appears to be in good health. If he skips two consecutive meals, call the veterinarian. Indeed, whenever a troublesome behavior or condition lasts longer than 24 hours, you should call your veterinarian. Before you do, take your Bully's temperature, because the veterinarian will want to know if it is elevated. Also be ready to let your veterinarian know if you have noticed any changes in your Bully's behavior recently, such as vomiting, diarrhea, listlessness, or drinking water more often than usual.

Lack of interest in food is not the only, or always the first, sign of illness. You should call your veterinarian if your Bulldog exhibits any of the symptoms listed in the checklist on page 80.

Do not worry about making a pest of yourself by calling your veterinarian whenever your Bulldog does not seem right. No concerned veterinarian will be put out by hearing from a concerned owner, no matter what symptom(s) he or she is reporting. Also, do not hesitate to seek another opinion if you have any reservations about the way your veterinarian is treating your Bulldog.

Breed Needs

There is no substitute for the counsel of a good veterinarian. No book or magazine article, no newsletter, longtime breeder, or Internet forum is a substitute for the diagnosis and prescription provided by a qualified veterinarian. When your Bulldog does not appear well, call your veterinarian first and tell him or her the symptoms that look troubling to you.

CHECKLIST

Troublesome Conditions

- ✔ Labored breathing
- ✔ Elevated temperature
- ✔ Persistent coughing, gagging, or sneezing
- ✔ Excessive drinking
- ✔ Repeated head shaking
- ✔ Runny, cloudy, bloodshot eyes
- ✔ Runny nose
- ✔ Pale or inflamed gums
- ✔ Seriously foul breath
- ✔ Digging at his ears
- ✔ Bodily swelling or abscess
- ✔ Scratching, licking, or chewing himself excessively
- ✔ Flea dirt in his coat or bed
- ✔ Worms or blood in his stool
- ✔ Blood in his urine
- ✔ Limping or altered gait
- ✔ Dragging his hindquarters across the floor
- ✔ Lethargic for more than a day
- ✔ Recurring vomiting during the last day
- ✔ Diarrhea for more than one day
- ✔ Excessive drooling

External Parasites

Parasites are living organisms that reside in or on other living organisms called *hosts*, feeding on blood, lymph cells, or tissue. Internal parasites dwell inside their hosts. External parasites live on the surface of their hosts.

The external parasites that can be found on a Bulldog include fleas, ticks, flies, lice, larvae, and mites. These insects and arachnids not only damage skin tissue but also transmit harmful bacteria and viruses to your Bully. In sufficient quantities external parasites can sap a Bulldog's energy, weaken his resistance to infection and disease, and saddle him with diseases and parasitic worms.

The signs of external parasites are flea dirt, skin lesions, pustules, hair loss, redness, dandruff, scaling, scabs, growths of thickened skin, or an unpleasant odor. If you notice any of these symptoms while you are grooming or petting your Bulldog—or if he begins to scratch or to bite at himself excessively—call your veterinarian. The earlier that external parasites are detected and confronted, the easier they are to control.

Waging War on Fleas and Ticks

There are countless shampoos, sprays, powders, mousses, roll-ons, drop-ons, flea collars, machines that make ear-piercing noises, and wonder dips "guaranteed" to kill fleas and, in some cases, ticks. The newest products in this brigade are the "spot-ons," which are applied once a month between your Bulldog's shoulders or at three or four spots along his back.

Most spot-ons dissolve into the oils of your Bully's skin and coat, then spread quickly over his entire body. One product, which is available only by prescription from your veterinarian, penetrates your Bully's skin and enters his bloodstream.

Most spot-on flea killers are safe for use with puppies six to eight weeks old and older. These products are also waterproof for up to 30 days, which means they are still effective after you have bathed your Bulldog.

Spot-on products are advertised to begin killing fleas within three to five minutes after they have bitten your dog and to kill between 98 and 100 percent of the fleas on your Bully within 12 to 24 hours, depending on the product. Some spot-ons kill only fleas, flea eggs, and larvae, whereas others kill ticks also. One product, which penetrates your Bully's skin, goes to work in his tissues and bloodstream to prevent heartworm disease as well. This product then migrates from the bloodstream into the skin to kill adult fleas, American dog ticks, and ear mites—and to prevent flea eggs from hatching. Finally, it also fights to expel parasitic worms.

Before selecting a product to use in the war against fleas and ticks, be sure to seek the advice of your veterinarian. She or he will help you to determine which product is suitable for your Bully.

Flea Collars Insecticidal flea collars do not light up the scoreboard with flea kills, and some dog owners are concerned that the pesticides in these collars can be harmful to a dog. If you choose to put a flea collar on your

HOME BASICS
Flea Prevention

To check your Bulldog for fleas, turn him over and inspect the area near his hind legs, where his coat is thinner. You may see a flea scurrying for cover. If you do not find any fleas but you do find specks of dirt on your Bully, put a small amount of that dirt on a paper towel and wet it. If the dirt turns red, it is flea dirt—flea excrement, to be exact, which derives its red color from your Bully's blood. If a visual inspection of your Bulldog does not reveal any suspects, run a flea comb through his coat for good luck.

If your Bulldog is crawling with fleas, bathe him with an anti-flea shampoo compatible with the anti-flea medication you have selected. Do not forget to wash your dog's bed and blankets and to vacuum the house thoroughly every other day until the flea invaders have been conquered. Cut a flea collar into several pieces and put it in your vacuum-cleaner bag to kill any fleas that wind up in there. Change the bag when it is only half full to prevent a flea colony from sprouting in the bag.

Bulldog, remove the collar from its sealed package and snap it taut a few times to get rid of excess insecticide. Wash your hands immediately. Let the collar air out away from pets and children for 24 to 36 hours before putting it on your Bulldog, then watch him closely for several days. If he breaks out in sores, if he seems groggy, or if he develops nasal irritation or inflamed eyes, remove the collar at once and contact your veterinarian. Flea collars that get wet must be removed and dried. Many flea collars are ineffective once they have been wet, and should be discarded.

The Field Some flea-fighting products have been around since the invention of the wheel, and the people who put their faith in these products swear that new-fangled anti-flea products are nothing more than a futile attempt to reinvent the wheel. Among the more popular low-tech flea fighters is diatomaceous earth, which is sprinkled into rugs and upholstery on the theory that it causes fleas to dry up

CAUTION

Humans, too, can be affected by some of their dogs' external parasites. In cases of severe flea infestation, fleas may hop onto humans for a take-out meal. Certain kinds of mites will migrate to humans, too, and so will ticks. Especially worrisome to humans are ticks that carry Rocky Mountain spotted fever and Lyme disease. The latter is the most common tick-borne disease in the United States.

and die upon contact. Salt and borax are also used for this purpose.

Brewer's yeast is added to a dog's food and dusted into his coat and bedding because fleas so dislike its flavor they will seek other animals to bite after they have gotten a taste of it. Garlic, added to a dog's food, and vinegar, which is added to his drinking water, are reputed to have the same effect.

Chelated zinc, lecithin, cod liver oil, cold-pressed, unsaturated vegetable oil, kelp, and vitamin C also are touted as flea remedies. Scientists and most veterinarians, however, are skeptical about the value of many of these remedies.

Sounding Off About Ear Mites

Ear mites are nothing if not adaptable. Several types of mites can invade and occupy the ear canals of dogs and cats, the same mite can affect both species, and ear mites can live anywhere on an animal's body. Left untreated, they can do painful damage to the ear canals and eardrums, and may cause permanent hearing loss.

If your Bulldog scratches or digs at his ears frequently, he may have ear mites. Ditto if he shakes his head as though he is uncomfortable or rubs his head against the carpet or a furniture leg. The presence of any or all of these symptoms warrants a call to your veterinarian, especially if you check your Bully's ears with a cotton swab first and dredge out what appears to be coffee grounds but is, actually, your Bulldog's dried blood.

Because ear mites spread rapidly among animals—though, fortunately, not among humans—you should attack them swiftly with an ear mite medication, either commercial or prescription, recommended by your veterinarian. Most of these medications contain an insecticide, usually pyrethrin, although ivermectin, fipronil, and selamectin also have been used to eradicate ear mites. Treatment usually lasts two to four weeks, depending on the medication.

Ear mites can live anywhere on a dog's body, so be sure to choose a flea-and-tick product that contains one of the above ingredients. If you have other pets, do not forget to monitor them and to begin treatment at the first sign of mites. In fact, some Bulldog owners prefer to treat all their dogs for ear mites if one dog has them.

Keeping Mangy Critters at Bay

Mange is a determined, contagious disease of the skin caused by mites living on a dog's skin, in his hair follicles, or, sometimes, under his skin. Dogs always have mites, but some mites, if they are allowed to persist untreated,

HOME BASICS
Ticking Time Bombs

There you are, settled comfortably in front of your 52-inch flat screen, hand draped idly over your Bully's shoulders, when you notice a lump on his skin that does not feel as though it ought to be there. You put the remote down and part your Bully's fur at the lump to see what the problem is.

That brings you face-to-face with one of nature's most disgusting marvels—a foul-looking, grayish lump that is the body of a tick swollen to obscene dimensions with the blood of your Bulldog. What do you do now? First hit the pause button on the remote, then proceed to your dog-supplies drawer and get the tick-removal tool you bought when you were shopping for puppy supplies.

Most tick-removal tools feature a hook that can be slid between the tick's face and your Bully's skin without poking a hole in the latter. After the hook has been eased into place, give your wrist a quarter turn upward and remove the tick.

What you do with the tick is your call. Fry it with a match, or place it inside a folded paper towel and squish it with a hard object. Be creative and be quick, then get some alcohol and clean the spot where the tick was attached to your Bully.

If you forgot to buy a tick-removal tool and you do not have a pair of Swiss Jeweler's Forceps #7 around the house, tweezers will do in a pinch, so will hemostats. Be careful not to poke your Bully or to leave the tick's head attached after you have removed its swollen, disgusting body. A bodyless tick is still capable of causing infection.

can cause reactions that create uncomfortable symptoms for your Bully: inflammation, itching, and loss of hair.

The three common types of mange that affect dogs are cheyletiella, sarcoptic, and demodectic mange. The mite that causes cheyletiella mange may be visible under a magnifying glass, but the mites that cause sarcoptic and demodectic mange are not.

The symptoms of cheyletiella mange include mild itching and the appearance of white flakes on the head, neck, and back. The symptoms of sarcoptic mange include body sores, vigorous itching, hair loss around the ears, elbows, and legs, and a dodgy odor. Symptoms of demodectic mange, which is most commonly seen in puppies between the ages of three and ten months, may include loss of hair on the face, head, and front legs.

The mites causing demodectic mange are transferred from the mother to her puppies, whose immune systems are often not mature enough to resist the mites. Demodetic mange does not itch as badly as sarcoptic mange does. In fact, demodectic mange may disappear on its own if it is not widespread

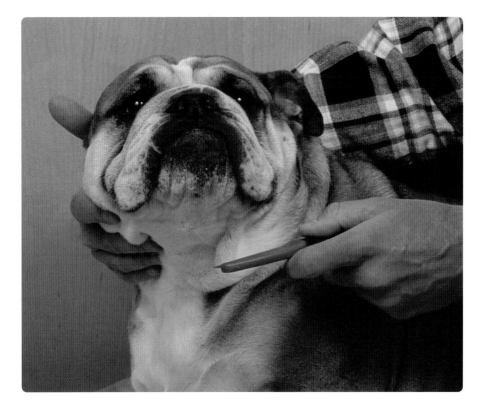

on a dog's body. If it spreads beyond a few small areas, treatment can be lengthy.

If you suspect your Bully has mange, consult your veterinarian. She or he will take a skin scraping to determine the type and the volume of mites present. This information is necessary in formulating a treatment strategy.

That strategy may include dips or medicated baths, topical ointments, or oral drugs. Topical treatments are most commonly used for localized cases of mange, whereas dips and shampoos are necessary if the disease has spread extensively. In the most severe cases of mange, the affected area of the dog may have to be shaved, and the dog may have to be isolated during treatment for the protection of any other dogs in the house.

Internal Parasites

Into each canine life a few worms must crawl. The four kinds of worms that can infest dogs are roundworms, tapeworms, hookworms, and whipworms. Stool-sample analysis will reveal the presence of roundworms and hookworms. Tapeworms, however, elude this method of investigation. They are best detected by the ancient Egyptian technique of peering studiously at a

FYI: Protozoa

Protozoa are another internal parasite to which a dog can play host. Protozoa are usually one-celled organisms that may contain specialized structures for feeding and locomotion. One protozoan sometimes found in dogs is *Toxoplasma gondii*, which is carried in oocysts shed in cat feces. If you have a cat, do not allow your Bulldog to go truffle hunting in the litter box. Fortunately, the threat of your Bulldog's being infected by *T. gondii* from your cat is limited. Once a cat's immune system responds to *T. gondii*, the cat stops shedding oocysts. Two other protozoan diseases are coccidia, which is usually found in young dogs kept in crowded conditions, and giardia, which is found in dogs exposed to dirty (or potentially contaminated) water or to infected dogs.

dog's anus. During this examination, the inspector is looking for small, white tapeworm segments that look, you will forgive the indelicacy, like rice. These segments also can be seen on freshly minted stools.

The presence of heartworms can be detected by blood-sample analysis. If your Bulldog is negative for heartworms, your veterinarian can prescribe preventive heartworm medication to keep him that way. If your Bulldog tests positive for heartworms, he will require treatment that may include hospitalization and/or surgery.

Most worms, despite their repugnance, are not difficult to control. When you acquire a Bulldog, ask the person from whom you get him when he (the Bulldog) was last dewormed and what deworming agent he was given. To be safe, take a stool sample and your new Bulldog's previous deworming history to your veterinarian. He or she will recommend a safe, effective deworming agent and will set up a deworming schedule.

Medicating and Feeding a Sick Bulldog

Ignorance is bliss when medicating a Bulldog. As long as the Bulldog remains ignorant of the contents of the mound of food you offer on a tablespoon or on the tips of your fingers, the pill hidden in that mound of food should go down blissfully. If your Bulldog is too sick to eat, you may have to administer pills manually or with a pill gun. The latter is available in a pet shop or from a pet-supply catalog. Either way the technique is the same: placing the pill as far back on your Bulldog's tongue as possible, holding his mouth shut, and stroking his throat—or blowing gently into his face—until he swallows. Do not forget to praise him when he does.

Bulldogs convalescing from an illness or injury must consume enough fluid to replace what they lose through elimination and panting. If your

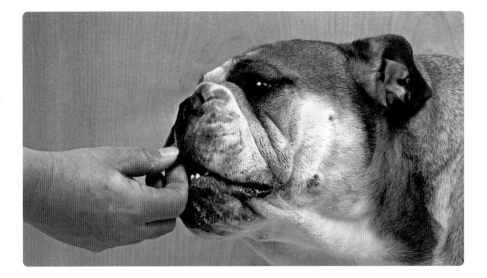

Bulldog is unwilling to drink, you will have to get nourishing liquids—water or broths—down his throat one way or another.

Spooning fluid into a Bulldog's mouth can be messy and uncomfortable for you and your dog. A syringe or a spray bottle is a better choice. Your veterinarian can tell you how much fluid your Bulldog should receive daily.

If your Bulldog is off his feed, switch to an all-canned-food diet and warm the food slightly in the microwave to release its aromas before giving it to him. Be sure to stir the warmed food and to test it for pockets of heat before offering it to your Bulldog.

When a Bulldog is not eating, virtually any food is nutritious food for the time being: baby food, turkey or chicken from the deli, canned dog food marinated in beef or chicken broth, hamburger seasoned with garlic, broth straight up, anything that will revive your Bulldog's interest in eating. (In serious cases you may have to feed your Bulldog a pureed diet with a large syringe.)

The Bulldog's Activity Schedule

Bulldogs, being the civilized and sensible creatures that they are, do not require much activity. They do enjoy being outdoors, however, and if at all possible should be provided with a securely fenced yard in which they can trundle about when the spirit moves them. They do not have to spend large amounts of time in the yard. Half an hour in the morning and another in the afternoon, temperature and weather permitting (with access to fresh water, of course), are sufficient. Bulldogs that live in houses or apartments without yards should be walked 10 or 15 minutes at least once a day (again, weather permitting)—this is in addition to their constitutional walks—and should be

BE PREPARED! Overheating

If your Bulldog begins to pant and slobber excessively after being in a hot environment, move him to a cool or air-conditioned room and take his temperature at once. If his temperature is elevated beyond 102°F (38.9°C), give him a little cold water to drink and then reduce his temperature slowly with a cool-water bath.

You should also have lemon juice on hand to squirt against the back of your Bulldog's throat. This will cut through the accumulated mucus, thereby helping him to breathe easier.

If your Bully's temperature reaches 106°F (41.1°C), he is verging on heatstroke, and you need to act quickly while keeping your wits about you. As before, offer him small amounts of water if he is alert and can drink, then bring his temperature down with a cool-water bath. Move his legs gently while he is in the bath to increase circulation. Check his temperature every 15 minutes until it falls below 103°F (39.4°C).

If your Bulldog collapses after you bring him in from the heat—or while you are attempting to moderate his temperature—get him to a veterinarian as quickly as possible. Secure an ice pack to your dog's belly before putting him into the car.

taken two or three times a week to an area where they can enjoy a little frolic under their owners' supervision.

Gifts often come with strings attached, and the Bulldog's modest activity needs are a case in point. Hot or humid weather are a challenge to a Bulldog's respiration system, which has been compromised for the sake of his pretty face. Bulldog owners, therefore, should have an accurate outdoor thermometer mounted somewhere near the yard. When the temperature reaches 80°F (27°C), do not leave your Bulldog outdoors for more than a few minutes. To do otherwise is to court heatstroke.

Heatstroke, which occurs when rectal temperatures spike to 109.4°F (43°C) or when they linger around 106°F (41°C), destroys cell membranes and leads to organ failures. The dehydration that accompanies heatstrokes thickens the blood, which deprives tissues of necessary oxygen. The muscles, kidneys, liver, and gastrointestinal tract also may be affected. Moreover, heatstroke can cause swelling and subsequent damage to the brain, blindness, hemorrhages, convulsions, and fatal seizures.

Bulldog Nutrition

You do not have to be a gourmet cook or command a gleaming arsenal of expensive cookware to feed your Bulldog a balanced, nourishing diet. Indeed, you do not have to know a dispensable amino acid from an indispensable one, or the number of amino acids a dog requires, to be a good

provider. All you need are a few coping strategies. These, of course, you can acquire by reading this chapter.

Dry, Semimoist, or Canned?

Dog food is not hard to find. Supermarkets, convenience stores, pet shops, feed-and-grain emporiums, discount-buying clubs, and veterinarians will gladly sell you all you need, and some of those places will even have someone carry it to the car for you. The tricky part, and it really is not all that tricky, is sorting your way through the boxes, bags, cans, and competing manufacturers' claims.

Dog food is available in three configurations: dry, semimoist, or canned. Dry food is less expensive, easier to store, and more convenient to use than is canned food. Dry food also helps to reduce dental plaque to some extent.

Canned (sometimes called *wet*) food is more tasty than dry food, may contain a larger proportion of meat than

CAUTION

Refrigerate the unused portion of a can of dog food and use it within a day or two. Do not leave canned food sitting in your Bully's bowl between meals, because canned food spoils quickly.

FYI: Does My Bully's Butt Look Big?

It is difficult to venture what any Bulldog should weigh without knowing something about his bone structure, muscle development, and height. According to the American Kennel Club breed standard for Bulldogs, "The size for mature dogs is about 50 pounds (22.7 kg), for mature bitches about 40 pounds (18.2 kg)": but instead of looking only at the scale to determine if your Bulldog exceeds or falls short of his desirable weight, look closely at your Bulldog. If you can see his ribs, he is too skinny. If you run your hand gently down his back from shoulders to tail and you feel the spinous processes that stick out along the spine, or if during the same inspection you can feel his hip bones, your Bulldog is too thin.

If your Bulldog has an hourglass figure or if you cannot feel his ribs, he is too fat. Additional bouquets of fat are likely to blossom on the brisket (the area below the chest and between the forelegs), the neck, the abdomen, and the point at which the tail meets the body. If any of these spots seems too well padded, perhaps your Bully is too well fed. If you cannot see your dog's ribs but can feel them without having to squeeze his sides, he is probably neither too fat nor too thin.

The Burdens of Excess Weight

Whether you acquire a 12-week-old flurry of feet and kisses or a mature adult, there is a direct relationship between what you put into your Bulldog's bowl and the quantity of muscle and fat he develops. There also is a relationship between your Bulldog's weight and his state of health. Although excess weight is wrongly blamed for causing everything from heart problems to dislocated kneecaps, there is no denying that too much weight is often a contributing factor—and is almost always a complicating one—in many health-compromising conditions.

In addition to aggravating locomotor problems, excess weight makes it more difficult for Bulldogs to dissipate heat in sultry weather, a problem already common to all members of the breed, fat or not. Moreover, dogs, like people, are subject to an increasing litany of troubles as they grow older, and Bulldogs that are overweight when the specter of old age comes calling are saddled with an unfair handicap in fighting disease and infirmity. It is difficult to specify the point at which a Bulldog's health could be compromised by surplus weight, but dogs that are more than 15 percent above their recommended weights are candidates for less food and more exercise.

Ideal Bulldog Growth Chart (1 year)

1 month = 6 lbs.	7 months = 42 lbs.
2 months = 10 lbs.	8 months = 44 lbs.
3 months = 16 lbs.	9 months = 46 lbs.
4 months = 24 lbs.	10 months = 47 lbs.
5 months = 34 lbs.	11 months = 48 lbs.
6 months = 38 lbs.	12 months = 50 lbs.

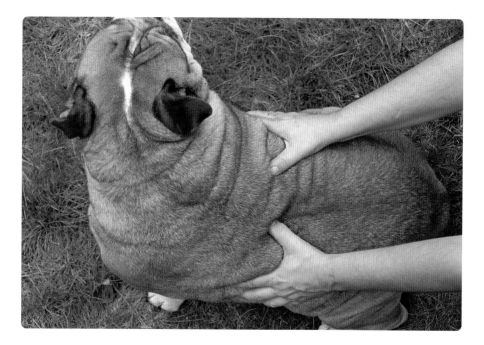

dry food, and, because it is 75 percent moisture, is a better source of water than other foods are. (Dry food contains roughly 10 percent water; semi-moist contains 33 percent.)

Semimoist food is the most expensive kind. It is frequently formed into pleasing shapes—and given a dye job—to increase its appeal to dog owners. Moreover, semimoist food contains sugar and, in some cases, flour. The only purpose these items serve is to help the food retain its faux-hamburger-patty shape.

Generic, Private Label, Regular, or Premium?

Besides having three categories of dog food from which to choose, you can select from generic, private-label, regular, or premium brands. Generic dog foods, which often do not carry a brand name, usually are produced and marketed close to where they are sold, thereby reducing transportation and purchasing costs. If, however, generic foods are produced from cheaper materials, they may not provide the nutritional quality of private-label, regular, or premium foods. Before buying a generic brand—or any brand of dog food—look for the nutritional-claim statement on the label and, just to be safe, buy only those foods whose claims of nutritional adequacy are based on Association of American Feed Control Officials (AAFCO) feed-trial procedures. AAFCO, the governing body for all animal-feed products, establishes guidelines and procedures for pet food manufacturers.

Private-label foods, which usually bear the house-brand name of a grocery-store chain, may be manufactured by the same companies that produce generic dog food, or they may be manufactured by nationally known companies that also produce their own, more recognizable brands. Instead of the traditional "Manufactured by . . ." statement that appears on the labels of generic, regular, or premium foods, private-label brands will contain one of the following statements: "Distributed by . . ." or "Manufactured for . . . ."

Regular brand dog foods are those with nationwide distribution and nationally recognizable names. Manufacturers usually make no special nutritional claims for regular dog foods, beyond, of course, the claims that they are good for your dog, promote strong bones, shiny coats, and healthier teeth, and meet AAFCO requirements.

Premium brands promise more. First, say manufacturers, the top-of-the-line processing techniques used in the production of premium foods reduce nutrient loss during heating. Moreover, premium foods, which can cost up to twice as much as regular brands, are made from higher-quality ingredients: chicken necks or backs instead of chicken by-products such as lung or bone. Indeed, the manufacturers of some premium foods boast that their products are made from human-grade ingredients. There is nothing in Bully's bowl that you could not eat yourself.

Premium foods contain no dyes, additives, or chemical preservatives, and because many premium foods are grain free, they are less likely to set off food allergies than are regular foods "supplemented" with cheap grain products. All this, manufacturers contend, results in foods with taste, smell, texture, and digestibility that are superior to other kinds of dog food.

Devotees of premium foods also claim that their higher digestibility results in lower fecal volume and less fecal odor. Premium-food manufacturers also claim that at the end of the day premium food costs no more to feed than regular does food because dogs eat less of premium than they do of regular food.

Finally, you should also be aware that premium dog foods do not have to meet higher standards than do regular foods. In fact, there is no special definition or standard by which the Food and Drug Administration or AAFCO judges premium food.

Weighing Nutritional Claims

Nutritional claims on dog food labels come in two varieties. In the first variety the manufacturer declares that Bowser Bits has been shown to provide complete and balanced nutrition in feeding trials conducted according to protocols established by AAFCO. To make this claim, a manufacturer must compare data obtained from an experimental and a control group of dogs, each of which must contain at least eight members.

The dogs in the experimental group are fed only Bowser Bits for a specified period of time. The control group is fed a diet already known to be complete and balanced. At the end of the test period, if the dogs fed Bowser Bits do not differ significantly along certain variables from the control group, the manufacturer is entitled to claim that Bowser Bits provides complete and balanced nutrition according to AAFCO's feed-trial protocols. The variables on which the experimental and control groups are compared include weight, skin and coat condition, red-blood-cell count, and other health measures.

To make the second kind of nutritional claim—that Bowser Bits was formulated to meet the levels established in AAFCO nutrient profiles—a manufacturer must sign an affidavit stating that he or she (or they) formulated Bowser Bits from ingredients that will contain, after they have been processed,

sufficient levels of all the nutrients AAFCO has determined a dog food should contain. The difference between buying a dog food that has been tested in feed trials and one that has been formulated to meet AAFCO profiles is like the difference between buying a preferred stock and a futures option: The consumer can be more confident that the preferred stock (the feed-tested dog food) is going to perform the way it is supposed to perform because it has been fed to real dogs in real feeding trials.

The meets-the-nutrient-profiles statement, on the other hand, is somewhat misleading. It does not mean that AAFCO has analyzed the food in question and has certified that it meets AAFCO standards. Nor does the statement necessarily mean that the manufacturer tested the food to determine

FYI: Preservative Free?

Because the regulations governing our food supply were written largely for the convenience of food producers rather than consumers, you cannot believe, much less trust, everything you read on a food label. For example, dog food manufacturers are not required by law to list preservatives that have been added already to the products they purchase to make dog food. Therefore, it is legal for a dog-food manufacturer to say that a food is "preservative free" even though he knows darn well that some of the ingredients he purchased to formulate that product contained preservatives. As long as a manufacturer does not add any preservatives to those already in his food's ingredients, he can say with a straight and legal face that his food is "preservative free."

If you choose to avoid chemical preservatives in favor of natural preservatives such as vitamin E, remember that natural preservatives do not last as long because they tend to break down when exposed to light and air. Buy naturally preserved foods in smaller quantities and be sure to store naturally preserved food in a cool, dark place.

whether it met AAFCO profiles. This statement simply means the manufacturer formulated the food from ingredients that should have provided enough nutrients to meet the AAFCO profile. We say "should have" because cooking always destroys nutrients in dog food to some extent. Therefore, the nutrients that go into the kettle are always present in greater amounts than the nutrients that go into the can.

Individual state regulators are responsible for checking the validity of nutritional claims. If a food is found wanting, the manufacturer is obliged to reformulate that food to provide sufficient levels of the nutrients that were lacking.

Some nutritional claims are conspicuous by their absence. Snack foods and treats do not have to contain any statement of nutritional adequacy. What is more, foods intended for intermittent or supplemental use only must be labeled so and should be used only on an intermittent basis.

Thus far we have discussed only one part of the nutritional claim made on dog food labels: the part that tells you the basis on which manufacturers state their claims. There is, however, a second part to nutritional statements: the part that specifies the dogs for which the food is intended. Thus, a complete nutritional claim for a feed-tested food will say: "Animal feeding tests using AAFCO procedures substantiate that Bowser Bits provides complete and balanced nutrition for all life stages of the dog." A complete nutritional claim for a meets-the-profile food will say: "Bowser Bits is formulated to meet the nutrient levels established by AAFCO nutrient profiles for all stages of a dog's life." Both these statements assure consumers that they can

HOME BASICS
Snack Time and Chew Toys

A considerable subset of the pet food industry is built on dogs' fondness for snacks and treats—and for humans' fondness for bribing their dogs into good behavior. Dog owners should remember, however, that snacks and treats are nutritionally deficient for full-time use.

You can feed some foods to your Bulldog all of the time and you can feed all foods to your Bulldog some of the time, but nutritional wisdom is the better part of knowing which time is which. Again, let the label be your guide. If the label says, "Bowser Beef Wellington Bits are intended for intermittent or supplemental use only," then use them intermittently. Do not allow snacks and treats to make up more than 5 to 10 percent of your dog's diet.

Chew toys are based on the principle that a dog's teeth are certified erogenous zones. Well aware of this fact, pet-supply manufacturers routinely paint, process, and press rawhide into "bones" for your dog's chewing enjoyment. Some rawhide bones are a bleached-looking white, others are an off-cream, and still others, which have been basted, Broasted, broiled, or roasted come in colors for which there are no words. In addition to being basted or Broasted, some bones are chicken, beef, hickory, cheese, peanut butter, or (for those Bulldogs expecting company) mint flavored. Because of its flexibility rawhide also can be fashioned into surreal approximations of tacos, lollipops, cocktail franks, bagels, french fries, and giant pretzels to appeal to human tastes.

There is the possibility that a dog can come to grief by chewing off pieces of rawhide and swallowing them. Be sure to monitor your Bulldog carefully the first few times you present him with a rawhide chew toy. If your dog shows an inclination to chew off pieces of the toy, give him something more substantial to chew on, such as a bone made of hard nylon, instead.

All chewables should be served inside the house. A Bulldog gnawing happily on a chewy treat in the backyard soon will be attended by a posse of ants, flies, bees if they are in season, and other uninvited hangers-on.

feed an all-life-stages food to their dogs from puppyhood through senior-hood, including motherhood, without worrying.

Instead of being formulated for all stages of a dog's life, some foods are intended for the maintenance of adult dogs only, and other foods are intended to support growth and reproduction. The latter are formulated to meet the increased nutritional needs of pregnant females and puppies. These foods must contain more of certain nutrients—more protein, calcium, phosphorus, sodium, and chloride, for example—than maintenance foods do. (Foods providing complete and balanced nutrition for all life stages of a dog also must meet growth-and-reproduction standards.)

Top Five Ingredients in Your Bulldog's Food

The list of ingredients on most dog-food labels is dizzying. Fortunately the ingredients are listed in descending order by volume. Therefore, the most important ingredients in any dog food are the first five on the ingredients list. These top-five ingredients tell you whether the food is worth its salt—or your money.

In a perfect world the top five ingredients in a dry dog food are a protein source such as chicken, turkey, beef, venison, or lamb—or chicken meal, meat meal, and so forth—and a carbohydrate source such as potatoes, sweet potatoes, or rice. In a less-than-perfect world, the top five ingredients in your Bulldog's dry food might be chicken meal, wheat flour, ground whole wheat, corn gluten meal, and rice bran.

Those last four items—wheat flour, ground whole wheat, corn gluten meal, and rice bran—are filler: stuff the manufacturer dumps into the food to increase its volume. There is nothing "wrong" with this practice, but some nutritionists worry that fillers may trigger allergic reactions if those fillers contain additives that dogs are not designed to eat.

The increased number of food allergy cases among dogs has led to the present trend toward grain-free dog foods or—at very least—toward the substitution of rice for corn, wheat, and soy grains, which are more likely to be harmful to dogs.

Breed Needs

Do Not Forget the Water

Water is the most important nutrient needed to sustain normal cell function. Therefore, dogs should have fresh water in a freshly cleaned bowl every day. Mammals can lose nearly all their reserves of glycogen and fat, half their protein stores, and 40 percent of their body weight and still survive. Adult dogs, composed of 60 percent water, are in severe metabolic disarray if they lose 10 percent of their body water, and death results if water loss rises to 15 percent.

The Role of Vitamins and Minerals

Dogs cannot reap the harvest from their food without the aid of vitamins, which combine with protein to create enzymes that produce hundreds of important chemical reactions. Vitamins also assist in forming hormones, blood cells, nervous-system chemicals, and genetic material.

Although dogs are mostly affected by the lack of vitamins, an excess of vitamins, especially A and D, also can be harmful. Vitamin A toxicity, the consequence of a liver-rich diet, causes skeletal lesions. Vitamin D toxicity, the upshot of unwarranted supplementation, results in calcification of the aorta, the carotid arteries, and the stomach wall.

If a commercial dog food is labeled nutritionally complete and balanced, do not add vitamins or supplements to it. Additional vitamins may upset the balance of vitamins already in the food and cause vitamin toxicity. The only dogs needing vitamin supplements are those not eating properly because of illness or those losing increased amounts of body fluids because of diarrhea or increased urination.

In addition to vitamins, dogs need the following 12 minerals: calcium, phosphorus, sodium, potassium, chloride, magnesium, iron, copper, zinc, manganese, iodine, and selenium. Minerals help to maintain tissue structure, fluid balance, and the body's acid-base (electrolyte) balance. Because mineral requirements are interrelated, the same warning about vitamin supplements applies to mineral supplements: Proceed with caution and only on your veterinarian's recommendation.

Feeding Schedule

The amount of food dogs require is determined by their age, condition, metabolism, environment, biological status, activity level, and ability to convert food into energy and heat. Variations in the effect of these factors among Bulldogs can make generalizations, not to mention feeding charts, something of a risk.

CAUTION

Chewables, like any other source of pleasure, also can be a source of pain. Chicken bones should be avoided entirely because they can splinter, get lodged in a dog's throat, or poke holes in his stomach or intestines. Also, if your Bully is fond of marrow bones or knuckle bones, roast them in a 175-degree oven for 20 minutes to kill any harmful bacteria.

If there is one generalization that can be made about weight, it is this: the amounts specified in feeding charts on dog food packages and cans are far too generous. Like the manufacturers of soap powder and shampoo, the makers of dog food usually overestimate the amount of their product a person needs to use in order to produce the desired results. The generosity on the part of dog food manufacturers is understandable. They would be embarrassed if dogs were to lose weight on the recommended amounts. Therefore, they recommend high.

During their first year, Bulldogs' food requirements diminish somewhat. Between three and six months of age, Bulldogs should eat three times a day. Many owners feed their dogs a mixture of dry and canned food, and many breeders recommend that because of a Bulldog's propensity for putting on weight quickly and the joint problems that that propensity can cause, Bulldog puppies should be fed a large-breed puppy food that has the proper ratio of calcium and phosphorus for growing bones.

At the three-to-six-month stage, a Bulldog should eat about ½ cup of dry food, marinated briefly in warm tap water, and a tablespoon of canned all-life-stages food at each meal. When they are six months old, Bulldogs can be fed twice a day, and each meal should consist of ½ cup of dry puppy food, marinated briefly in warm tap water, and a tablespoon or so of canned food.

When they are a year old, Bulldogs can be fed once a day if that is more convenient for their owners, or, as Bulldogs would no doubt prefer, they can be fed twice daily. Whatever the case, the daily food intake should consist of roughly ¾ cup of water-marinated dry food and a tablespoon or two of canned food.

Special Diets

Dogs are put on special diets for several reasons: illness, old age, or obesity among them. Dogs with hypertension, heart disease, or edema (swelling) should be on low-sodium diets. Dogs with kidney or liver conditions should be fed diets that contain moderate levels of high-quality protein and are low in phosphorus and sodium. Dogs that are underweight or that suffer from pancreatic or liver disease should be fed highly digestible food that is low in fat. If any of these or other conditions are diagnosed by a veterinarian, he or she may recommend a special diet. You should follow the veterinarian's instructions faithfully, and, of course, never feed a special diet to a Bulldog without first consulting a veterinarian.

In addition to special diets for sick dogs, several companies produce senior-citizen foods for older dogs. These foods are based on two principles: Older dogs need less of certain nutrients—proteins, phosphorus, and salt, for example—than younger dogs; and older dogs are less able to tolerate nutrient excess than younger dogs.

The jury and animal research are still out on the question of senior foods. It certainly cannot hurt to feed an older dog a senior food—which still must satisfy maintenance requirements to make the complete-and-balanced claim—but there is not yet enough evidence to show that senior foods help older dogs in any significant manner.

Other special foods have been formulated to sculpt the overweight dog into a fit-and-trim specimen. Diet dog food, usually called "lite," allows you to feed the same amount of food while lowering a dog's caloric intake. Lite food contains 20 to 33 percent fewer calories than regular food. Like other special diets, lite food should be fed only to those dogs for whom veterinarians recommend such diets.

The Home-Cooking Challenge

For many people, feeding their dogs is a near-religious experience involving Zen-like preparation and adherence to detail. Most home cooks insist that their dogs would not be as healthy, sparkling, stress resistant, and economical to feed on a commercial diet. They have the economical part right. Ground meat bought from a pet food provisioner is much less expensive than anything that comes in a box, pouch, or can.

Helpful Hints

If at any point in your Bulldog's life you decide to feed him a different kind of food than the one he has been eating, add that new food to his previous food in a ratio of one part new to three parts old. Every three or four days increase the new food while decreasing the old until the changeover is complete.

Whether raw meat—sometimes cooked and always infused with vitamins, minerals, oils, and other molecular talismans—is better than commercial food is questionable. Because meat is deficient in calcium, copper, and vitamins A, D, and E, anyone feeding dogs a diet based on raw meat must add the right vitamins and minerals in the right proportions.

This is more complex than pouring calcium, a few tablespoons of vitamins, and some brewer's yeast into the meat and mixing thoroughly. How much calcium must you add to raw meat to restore the calcium-phosphorus ratio to its optimal 1:1 to 2:1 range?

How do you convert the 10,000 units of vitamin X per pound listed on the label of a 20-ounce jar of dog vitamins into the proper amount that should be added to a pound of raw meat?

Which vitamin additive is the most balanced and complete? Does it also contain the proper minerals in the proper amounts and ratios?

Unless you have some special intuition or knowledge that dog food manufacturers with their million-dollar budgets and their battalions of feeding-trial dogs have overlooked, you should leave the nutritional driving to commercial pet foods. More than 90 percent of dog owners do.

Chapter Seven

Training and Activities

Many discussions of dog training begin with the observation that dogs are pack animals and that in the wild each dog pack has a leader to whom all other members of the pack defer. These discussions then advise that if we want our dogs to be well trained, we have to be ready to assume the role of pack leader in their lives.

Canine pack leaders have an easy life compared to human pack leaders, however, for in the wild the rules of the pack are simple: Higher-ranking members of the pack eat first, and the alpha male calls the tune during mating season. Otherwise all that new members of the pack have to learn is to move on when the alpha female—who is usually the boss dog in the pack—wants to move on and to curl up for the night when she decides.

Human pack leaders ask a bit more of a dog. Humans want their dogs to come when they are called, to sit when they are told, to stay where they are placed, to relieve themselves only outdoors, and so on. Unfortunately the all-powerful, wild-canine-pack leaders are not much help with these lessons, but the training principles introduced in this chapter will provide that help. They are based on your Bulldog's instinctive inclination to follow the leader, and they explain how you can use that inclination to shape your Bully's behavior, making him a happy, well-adjusted member of his new pack.

Breed Truths

Most Bulldogs are ready to start obedience training when they are six months old. Some may be ready a bit sooner; others not so soon. Because larger breeds like the Bulldog can be a challenge as they mature, especially if they possess the male Bully's gung-ho spirit, you and your Bully might benefit from attending puppy kindergarten obedience classes.

Ten Indispensable Training Tips

No matter what you want to teach your Bulldog—from a basic sit to a 30-minute down—you can make that lesson easier for you to teach and for him to understand if you employ these 10 indispensable training tips.

1. Conduct training sessions in a quiet place free from interruptions.
2. Limit each training session to roughly 10 minutes.
3. Give a command just once. If you keep repeating *"Sit"* until your Bulldog finally decides to sit, you are teaching him that the first *"Sit"*—or the first 10 *"Sits"*—can be ignored.
4. Do not use the same word or phrase to mean different things. If *"Down"* means to lie down, do not say *"Down"* when you want your Bully to get off the couch. Use *"Off"* or *"Scram"* or some other word instead.
5. Do not scold your Bulldog during training. When he makes a mistake, simply show him what you want him to do.
6. Choose a release word to let your Bulldog know when a command is concluded and he can relax. Release words come in a variety of flavors: *"OK," "Cool," "Awesome,"* and so on. Be sure to use the same release word from lesson to lesson. Do not use *"OK"* one day and *"You rock"* the next. Dogs thrive on consistency.
7. Do not train your Bulldog if you are irritable or angry. Losing your temper will make you feel guilty and your Bully feel anxious.
8. A training session is not over until you say it is. If your Bully tries to bolt, do not call him. Snap a leash on his collar and guide him back to class, or pick him up and carry him back if necessary.
9. If your Bulldog is not catching on to a lesson, ask yourself what you are doing wrong. Are you going too quickly? Are you handling your Bulldog too roughly? Do you sound impatient? Are you rewarding your Bulldog as soon as he does the right thing?
10. End each training session on a positive note. If your Bully is not making progress with a new command, go back to a command he knows and end the lesson with that—or guide him through the new lesson manually, give him a treat and lots of praise, then dismiss class.

Helpful Hints

Before you can sell a command to your Bulldog, you have to sell it to yourself. If you do not believe that he can master a command, or that you can teach it successfully, the two of you might as well watch a training video together for all you will accomplish teaching that command.

ACTIVITIES Reinforcing Good Behavior

After your Bulldog begins to respond regularly to a command, do not give him a food reward every time he does. If he knows he can get a treat whenever, he may decide on occasion that it is more rewarding to continue what he was doing, even if he was doing nothing, than to get that same old treat. If he does not get a treat every time, however, he will be more likely to obey every time because he always will be hoping that this time is the charm.

This maybe-yes-maybe-no technique is known as positive intermittent reinforcement. In order for it to work effectively, the reinforcement schedule must not be predictable. If you withhold the treat every third time your Bulldog obeys a command, he will soon begin timing his refusals to coincide with the empty hand. To be effective, intermittent reinforcement must be random. If your training sessions consist of four or five practices of a command during two or three sessions a day, withhold the treat the second time you give that command during the first session, the fourth time during the second session, and so on.

Do not be intermittent with your praise. You do not want your Bulldog thinking that you love him less for some performances than for others. Every time he obeys a command, say "Good boy" with great enthusiasm, even if you do not give him a treat.

The Food Connection

The use of food as a dog-training aid was once a controversial topic, and there are still trainers who equate using food to train a dog with paying students to perform well in school. No one argues, however, that food treats make initial training more interesting for your dog and less challenging to you.

If you decide to use food rewards to train your Bully, after you have taught him to sit, stay, come, and so on, use food as an occasional reward only. There may come a time when your Bully is about to wander off into trouble and you will want him to return to you even though you do not have a dog biscuit up your sleeve.

Basic Commands

Bulldogs make better companions if they have been trained to heed certain commands. The list is not lengthy, but it is virtually non-negotiable. You will enjoy your Bully more and he will enjoy life more if he is able to walk quietly on a leash, come when you call him, sit when he is told, and stay where you put him. These abilities make all the difference between a dog that

spends most of his time in the backyard because he is such a pistol in public and one who is able to enjoy many of the wonders beyond the yard.

Leash Walking

After your Bulldog puppy has been introduced to a collar and/or harness (see "Introducing the Collar or Harness," page 64), you can begin training him to walk on a leash attached to one of those devices. This part of his training can begin as soon as he is old enough to go for walks with you in public as part of his socialization process (see "Puppy Socialization Strategies," page 52). Like charity, however, leash training should begin at home.

When your Bully is comfortable with a collar or a harness, attach a 6-foot (1.8-m) leash to it. Allow him time to investigate the leash and to drag it around for a while, but, if necessary, discourage him from chewing it.

During this—or, perhaps, a subsequent—leash-wearing session, take your end of the leash in your left hand and follow your puppy wherever he wants to go for a minute or two. Do not allow him much more freedom than that or he might think he is supposed to walk you.

As soon as your Bully is unconcerned about your being at the end of his leash, it is time for you to take over the controls. Stand 1 or 2 feet (30–60 cm) in front of your Bully, holding the leash in your left hand and a treat in your right. Show him the treat and urge him to follow you as you back up three or four steps. If he does, stop, praise him, and give him the treat. After he has inhaled the treat, show him another one and encourage him to follow you a few more steps to get it. After he has followed you for three or four treats, end the session. Repeat this exercise two or three times a day for several days, and your Bully will soon be following you like a young kid follows an ice cream truck.

At that point begin withholding the treat occasionally—and making your Bully follow you for more than three or four steps when you do reward him with a treat. Eventually you can eliminate the use of treats when you begin taking your Bully for walks in public, where there are other sounds, sights, and scents to occupy his attention, but remember to bring along a few treats just in case.

Helpful Hints

While training your Bully to walk on a leash, do not tug on it as though it were a tow rope and he were a small truck stuck in the mud.

If during your at-home leash-walking lessons your Bully decides that he wants a turn at being the lead dog, let him wander almost to the end of the leash, then turn around without saying anything and walk the other way. When he reaches the end of the leash, he will realize you are missing and will turn to catch up with you. (Do not attempt this maneuver if your Bully is moving away from you at warp speed, as he might turn an unscheduled cartwheel when he gets to the end of the leash.)

Gather up your leash as he comes alongside, and praise him for whatever time he walks by your side, even if it is only a few seconds, before giving him a treat. He will learn soon that the only way he can keep an eye on you and your never-ending supply of treats is to stay by your side where he can see you.

A few Bulldogs have been known to ignore this turn-about correction. If yours is one of them, try a little off-leash warm-up. Grab a handful of dog treats, give one to your Bulldog, put the rest in your left hand, and keep that hand close to your body. If your Bully nips or paws at your treat hand, bump him lightly on the nose with the back of that hand to let him know he is not getting those treats for free.

Say "*Heel*" and begin walking. Your Bully will be right behind you, looking for another handout. Stop and praise him and pop a treat into his mouth every few yards. Keep your treat hand close to your side. When you give him a treat, do not move your hand away from your body. Make him move in close to get the treat. After playing this game for a few days, begin to practice leash walking again.

Come

The *come* and the *sit* commands are the most useful tactics in your obedience-training game plan. If you never teach your Bulldog anything else, teaching him to come when you call and to sit when he is told will reinforce your position as pack leader and his position as follower. You can tell him to sit for a treat, to sit at the doorway while you leave the room first, to sit while you put on his leash, to sit while a friend pets him. The possibilities are nearly infinite.

Begin while your Bulldog—let's say his name is Bronco—is in the same room as you but is not sitting on your lap. Call his name from no more than 2 or 3 feet (60–90 cm) away, add the word *"Come,"* and hold out a treat where he can see it.

"Come" probably will not mean anything to Bronco, but at the sound of his name and the scent of the treat, he should hustle toward you. If he does, praise him and give him the treat. A few minutes later, repeat this routine.

If Bronco ignores you when you call him, put the treat in your pocket and begin to leave the room. Bronco may start to follow you at that point. Praise him if he does to let him know he did something right, but do not give him the treat.

Practice this command several times a day for several days, and Bronco will come every time you call; but what good is it if he comes only when you call him in the television room or wherever you taught him that command? It is time to try this game in another location.

Try calling Bronco from a distance of 5 or 6 feet (1.5–1.8 m) in the backyard. If he ignores you, put a leash on him and lead him to the spot from which you called him, then praise him and give him a treat. Sure, it is a bit of a bribe to give him a treat at this point, but no one is looking; besides, entire countries are run on the principle of bribes.

CAUTION

If your dog is elderly or has arthritis, pushing down on his hindquarters, even gently, may be uncomfortable for him.

When Bronco is reliable about coming when he is called both off leash and out of doors, you can test his willingness to respond by calling him when he is doing something that might be more interesting than rushing to see what it is you want. Try calling him, for example, when he is sniffing at something in the grass that only he can smell or appreciate. If he comes, praise him, give him a treat, and let him go back to that spot in the grass. If he blows you off, put a leash on him and lead him to the spot from which you called him, then praise him and give him a treat before releasing him.

After you have trained Bronco to come when you call, do not untrain him by calling him when you want to scold him or to give him a bath or to lay some other grief on him. If he gets the idea that all rainbows do not end in a pot of gold, he will soon stop believing in rainbows. When Bronco is doing something you would rather he did not—rooting around in the trash, for example—call him, but do not scold him when he comes. Praise him and reward him, take him into the house, then go out and pick up the trash.

Sit

To teach your Bulldog to sit, first get his attention by kneeling in front of him with a treat in your right hand. If he shows any interest in the treat—which should be held just out of reach and slightly above his nose—give the sit command then push down gently and immediately on his hindquarters with your left hand or else scoop his hind legs under him, folding him into a sitting position. When he is sitting, praise him lavishly and give him that treat if you wish.

Practice the *sit* command three or four times during several training sessions a day. If your Bully resists the idea of sitting, fold him into a sitting position as you did before. You will know he has mastered the command when you can tell him to sit while you are standing up and he sits down as soon as he is told. When that day comes, you can begin teaching Bronco to sit while he is walking on a leash.

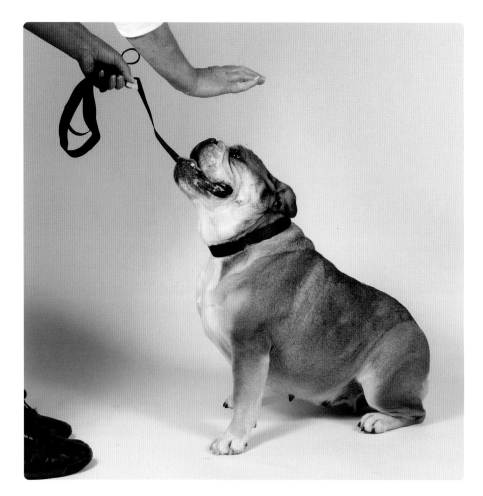

Begin by walking him on your left side with the leash in your left hand as usual, then come to a halt. When you do, say "*Sit.*" If he sits, great. If he hesitates, switch the leash to your right hand and pull up slightly while, at the same time, you press down gently on his rump with your left hand. After he sits down, praise him quietly, but control your enthusiasm. You want him to remain sitting, so if he stands up, repeat the *sit* command.

Stay

After Bronco has mastered the *sit* command, you can begin teaching him to stay. With Bronco standing in front of you on a leash, give him the *sit* command, then place your right hand—palm toward Bronco—about 6 inches (15 cm) in front of his face. Tell him "*Stay.*"

If he attempts to stand, pull the lead, which is in your left hand, straight up gently to keep him in place. If he succeeds in standing anyway, return him to the sitting position manually, take up your original place in front of Bronco, and try the *stay* command again.

Bronco should get the idea after one or two additional tries. When he does, silently count to five and release him by saying *"OK."* Then—and only then—praise him and give him a treat if you wish. Do not praise him while you are still standing in front of him or else he'll break the stay faster than a politician will break a campaign promise.

As Bronco is getting more skillful about staying, begin a new application of this command by walking him on a leash for several paces, then telling him to sit. After he does, give him the *stay* command while you are standing beside him, then walk forward, leading off with your right foot, until you have taken five steps. Turn and face Bronco.

If he has learned his lessons well, he will remain sitting until you call him or walk back to him. If he has followed you instead, take him back to his original position, put him in a *sit*, and repeat the exercise; but this time after giving the *stay* command, take only two or three steps before turning to face him.

Down

The *down* command is taught with the leash on. Begin by placing Bronco at your left in the *sit* position. Stoop, bend, crouch, or kneel alongside him— whichever is most comfortable—and hold a treat in front of his nose. As soon as he shows interest in the treat, move it slowly down and away from him in an arcing L shape. As you do, say *"Down."*

Breed Truths

If you are thinking about adopting an older Bulldog, do not hold his age against him. Despite an undeserved reputation for not being able to learn new tricks, older dogs can be easier to train than puppies. Any Bulldog who has reached the age of five, for example, has probably learned what *"No"* means. In addition, his attitude toward life is more easygoing than it was when he was a puppy, and therefore he is better able to concentrate on his lessons.

Obedience training with a recently acquired older Bulldog is a good way to establish a bond between dog and owner. The old sport will thrive on the attention, and the owner, especially if he is an old sport himself, will identify with his buddy's progress.

Unless Bronco is seriously ill, he will lunge for the treat. If he stands up when he does, withdraw the treat, put him in the *sit* position once again, and repeat the exercise. This time lean your left arm across his back to keep him from rising and to inspire him to stretch his front feet forward into the *down* position as he lunges for the treat. If he stands up or does anything but assume the *down* position, withdraw the treat, put him in the *sit* position, and try again.

You may have to try this exercise several times before you finally get Bronco where you want him. After you do, be sure to praise him and to give him the treat. Make sure that he consumes the treat in the *down* position, then release him and praise him again.

Turn

Dog training does not always have to have a practical purpose. Sometimes you may want to teach your Bully a trick just because you can—and because he can master it. The *turn* is one of those tricks.

Begin with your Bulldog standing up facing you. Let him see that you have a treat in your right hand, then say *"Turn."*

Hesitate a second, then holding your right hand just far enough from your Bully so he cannot get the treat, move your hand in a counterclockwise circle above and around your Bully so that he has to turn around completely as he follows the treat. When he is facing you again, praise him and give him the treat. (If your arm is not long enough to teach this trick comfortably, tie the treat to the end of a dowel and use it to lead your Bully around in a circle. Reward him with a treat out of your pocket if he makes a circle correctly.)

Repeat this exercise several times a day for several days. When you notice that your Bully begins to turn as soon as he hears the word *turn*, do not move the treat. If he completes the circle on his own, praise him happily and give him the treat.

If he stops in midcircle and comes back looking for his treat, pet him calmly but do not give him the treat; then say *"Turn"* again and move the treat in a circle for him to follow. Eventually he will get the idea, and he will have learned his first party trick.

The Canine Good Citizen Test

The Canine Good Citizen (CGC) test is an American Kennel Club (AKC)-sponsored certification program designed to promote canine good manners at home and in the community. CGC tests are administered at a nominal cost—usually $10 or $15—by dog clubs, AKC judges, 4-H leaders, therapy-dog evaluators, veterinarians, veterinarary techs, groomers, private trainers, kennel owners, and animal control and police K-9 officers. When you are ready to have your dog tested, check with one of those sources or visit the following AKC web page, *akc.org/events/cgc/cgc_bystate.cfm*, to find an evaluator in your area.

Dogs that successfully complete the CGC test are eligible to receive a Canine Good Citizen certificate from the AKC. With a little help from a friend or two, you can home-school your Bulldog for the CGC, or you can sign up for CGC classes at a kennel club.

The CGC test comprises ten individual sections:

1. Accepting a friendly stranger. The evaluator greets the handler in a friendly manner. The dog may not approach the evaluator, nor may it act resentful or shy.
2. Sitting politely for petting. The evaluator pets the dog, who is sitting at his handler's side. The dog may stand up as he is being petted, and his handler may talk to him throughout the exercise, but the dog must not exhibit shyness or resentment.

3. Appearance and grooming. Using the handler's comb or brush, the evaluator grooms the dog briefly, examines his ears, and picks up each front foot. The dog need not hold a specific position during this process, and the handler may talk to and encourage the dog.

4. Out for a walk. The dog may be on either side of the handler. The evaluator may use a preplotted course or may direct the dog-and-handler team verbally. The "walk" should include a left turn, a right turn, and an about-face—with at least one stop in between and another at the end. The handler may talk to the dog along the way, praise him, or give commands in a normal tone of voice.

5. Walking through a crowd. The dog and handler walk around—and pass close to—at least three people. The dog may show some interest in them, but he should stay with his handler and not display over-exuberance, shyness, or resentment. The handler may talk to the dog, encouraging him or praising him, throughout the test.

6. *Sit* and *down* on command, and staying in place. The dog's leash is replaced with a 20-foot (6-m) line. Then the handler gives the dog the *sit* and *down* commands, touching the dog if necessary to offer guidance. At the evaluator's instruction, the handler tells the dog to stay in either the *sit* or the *down* position, then walks forward the length of the line, turns, and walks back to the dog. The dog must remain where he was left, though he may change position, until the evaluator tells the handler to release the dog.

7. Coming when called. After telling the dog to stay or to wait—or giving no command at all—the handler walks 10 feet (3 m), turns to face the dog, then calls him. The handler may then encourage the dog to come.

8. Reaction to another dog. Two handlers and their dogs approach each other from a distance of roughly 20 feet (6 m). The handlers stop, shake hands, exchange pleasantries, then continue on for about 10 feet (3 m). The dogs should show no more than casual interest in each other.

9. Reaction to distraction. The evaluator presents two distractions—dropping a chair, a crutch, or a cane, rolling a crate dolly past the dog,

BE PREPARED! CGC Supplies

When your Bulldog takes the Canine Good Citizen test, you will be required to have with you the following:

- Proof of rabies vaccination
- A brush or a comb
- A buckle or training collar
- A 6-foot (1.8-m) leash

or having a jogger run in front of the dog. The dog may express some interest and curiosity and may even appear lightly startled, but he should not panic, try to run away, show aggressiveness, or bark. The handler may talk to the dog and encourage or praise him during the exercise.

10. Supervised separation. The handler gives the dog's leash to the evaluator and walks out of sight of the dog, who is expected to remain with the evaluator for three minutes. The dog does not have to stay in one position, but he should not continually bark, whine, or pace, or show anything stronger than mild agitation or nervousness. The evaluator may talk to the dog but should not engage in excessive talking or petting.

Rally

If your Bulldog earns a Canine Good Citizen certificate and is looking for new worlds to conquer, rally is the next step. It is more rigorous than the CGC test, but less formal than obedience competition and less physically demanding than agility trials, for which Bulldogs as a tribe are not so well suited as are some more athletic breeds.

In rally competition dog-and-handler teams complete a predetermined course comprising 10 to 20 stations, the exact number depending on the level of the competition—rally novice, rally advanced, or rally excellent. Each station is marked with a sign that provides instructions about the command to be executed there. These commands may require a dog to sit or to lie down as his handler walks once around him; to turn with his handler 270 or 360 degrees to the right or to the left; to walk at a fast or slow pace to the next station; to halt, stand briefly, and then lie down; to back up three steps from a halt; to jump a barrier; to weave between pylons and so on.

Before competition begins, handlers may walk the course without their dogs to familiarize themselves with its requirements. A copy of the course is posted at ringside so that exhibitors know what to expect and where to go once they are in the ring.

At the "forward" command from the judge, a dog-and-handler team sets off on the course, moving briskly but normally. The dog must be under the control of the handler at his left side as they go. Each performance is timed, but times count only in case of a tie.

Handlers are permitted unlimited communication with their dogs, including talk, praise, encouragement, hand claps, leg pats, and so on. A handler may not touch his dog, however, nor may the handler use loud or harsh commands or intimidating signals.

In the rally novice class the dog remains on leash at all times while completing 10 to 15 exercises. In the rally advanced class all exercises are performed off leash, and the course consists of 12 to 17 stations, including at least one jump. In the rally excellent class the dogs are off leash entirely except for the "honor" exercise, during which a dog must remain in the *sit* or *down* position at the judge's direction while another dog-and-handler team completes the course. The rally excellent course comprises 15 to 20 stations and at least two jumps. At this level a handler may not clap or pat his leg to encourage his dog.

A few examples of the infractions for which a dog can be penalized during a rally competition include touching a jump, pylon, post, or person; barking excessively; hitting a jump; performing a station incorrectly; or eliminating on the course.

AKC rally trials are open to all dogs at least six months of age who are registered with the AKC or listed with the AKC Purebred Alternative Listing/ Indefinite Listing Privilege or recorded with the Foundation Stock Service.

Therapy Work

So great is the Bulldog's spirit that it seems a pity not to share that spirit with others. Some Bulldog owners choose to do this by training their Bullies for therapy work. In a hospital or nursing home therapy dogs may either make the rounds to be petted by residents or take part in a patient's care by retrieving a toy thrown by that patient.

Therapy dogs also visit schools, where they serve as attentive, nonjudgmental listeners while children read to them. Because Bulldogs are so reliable with children, they are excellent candidates for this job.

Before you and your Bully go charging off to the nearest school or nursing home, contact the Delta Society ([425] 679-5500 or *deltasociety.org*) or Therapy Dogs International ([973] 252-9800 or *tdi-dog.org*) to find out how your Bully can become a registered therapy dog by passing a test similar to the Canine Good Citizen test.

The therapy dog test includes exercises in which a dog interacts with a person using a wheelchair, crutches, a walker, or all three. Your Bully does not need this certificate in order to serve as a therapy dog, but his chances of being accepted—and the chances of his therapy visits going more smoothly—are enhanced by formal training.

Helpful Hints

Obedience titles are earned at obedience trials, which are usually held in conjunction with conformation shows. A Bulldog must be six months old to compete in an obedience trial. Entry fees for obedience are roughly $25. Entry forms can be obtained from the American Kennel Club website, *www.akc.org/pdfs/AEN999.pdf*, or from a dog show superintendent (see "Resources," page 180).

Obedience Trials

Most Bulldog owners would be satisfied with a Canine Good Citizen certificate or, perhaps, a rally title or two. Other folks, however, might want to press on—or skip these activities altogether—and enter their dogs in an obedience trial.

The differences among the CGC test, rallies, and obedience trials are a matter of kind as well as degree. Obedience trials include more advanced commands such as jumping, retrieving, and scent discrimination, and the rules in obedience trials are more strict. You may give your dog a command only once in an obedience trial, and you may not talk to him or otherwise encourage him after you do. Moreover, during an obedience trial your dog must walk next to you—both on and off leash—in a formal *heel* position as if he and you were joined at the leg by an invisible wire.

Novice Class

This is the entry-level obedience class, in which your Bully can earn the Companion Dog (CD) title by receiving a qualifying score in three different competitions from three different judges. A qualifying score is awarded if a dog earns at least 50 percent of the points available in each obedience exercise and if the total number of points he earns is at least 170 out of possible 200. The following exercises are required in the novice obedience class:

- Heel on leash and figure eight—The handler is instructed to move his dog forward; to turn right or left; to move at a fast, slow, or normal pace; and to halt. During the figure-eight test, dog and handler weave around and between two ring stewards standing 6 feet (1.8 m) apart.
- Heel free—Same requirements as heel on leash, but without the leash.
- Stand for examination—The handler removes his dog's leash and walks away from him; the dog remains standing as the judge examines him briefly.
- The recall—After telling his dog to *sit* and then to *stay*, the handler walks about 35 feet and turns to face him. At the judge's signal the handler calls the dog, who should move briskly toward the handler and sit in front of him. At the judge's next signal, the handler tells the dog to *finish*—circle behind the handler and assume the heel position at the handler's left side.
- The long sit—All dogs and handlers line up in a row. After telling their dogs to *sit* and then to *stay*, the handlers walk across the ring and turn to face them. A minute later the handlers return to their dogs, who are, theoretically, still sitting where their handlers left them.
- The long down—Same as the long sit except the dogs must remain in the *down* position for three minutes.

CAUTION

If you decide to compete for titles in any competition, obedience or otherwise, in which your Bully will be required to jump, have him examined by a veterinarian first to determine if his (your Bully's) joints are up to the task.

Open Class

In this class, which is open to all dogs who have earned a CD certificate, your Bully can earn the Companion Dog Excellent (CDX) title. Once again he must receive a qualifying score in three different competitions from three different judges. The following exercises are required in the open obedience class:

- *Heel* and figure eight off leash.
- Drop on recall—A handler puts his dog in the *stay* position, walks 35 feet (10.5 m), turns, then calls the dog. As he approaches the handler, the dog drops into the *down* position at the handler's signal. The handler then calls the dog again, and he finishes the recall.

- Retrieve on flat—The handler instructs his dog to *sit* at his side. The handler then throws a dumbbell; the dog remains sitting until he is told to retrieve it.
- Retrieve over high jump—A dog retrieves a dumbbell thrown over a jump that is, for Bulldogs, about 12 inches (30 cm) high.
- Broad jump—A dog jumps a distance equal to twice the height of the high jump.
- Long sit—A dog must remain sitting for three minutes while his handler is out of the ring and out of sight.
- Long down—A dog remains in the *down* position for five minutes while his handler is out of the ring and out of sight.

Utility Class

This class, which some dog owners refer to as "futility," is open to all dogs who have earned a CDX title. In utility a Bulldog can earn the Utility Dog (UD) title. Once again he must receive a qualifying score in three different competitions from three different judges. The following exercises are required in the utility class:

- Signal exercise—a dog must respond correctly to his handler's signal to *come*, *stand*, *sit*, *stay*, and *down*. No voice commands are permitted.
- Scent discrimination—A dog must retrieve from two groups of articles (one comprising leather items, the other metal) the one item in each group that bears his owner's scent.
- Directed retrieve—Dog and handler are presented with a row of three gloves. The judge indicates which glove he wants the dog to retrieve and then return to the handler; the handler then directs the dog, using a hand signal only, to fetch that glove.
- Moving stand and examination—The dog *heels* beside his handler until, at the judge's direction, the handler commands the dog to stand while he, the handler, continues walking another 10 to 12 feet (3–3.6 m), then turns to face the dog. After the judge examines the dog briefly; his handler calls him to the *heel* position.
- Directed jumping—The handler tells his dog to move away from him. After the dog has complied with that command and is sitting facing his handler, the judge indicates which of two jumps the dog must clear before returning to his handler. The handler then directs the dog to clear that jump. The process is repeated for the other jump.

Beyond the Recall of Duty

If you have the inclination and your dog has the interest, he may continue to compete in the open and utility classes after he has won his Utility Dog title. At that point he will be chasing the UDX (Utility Dog Excellent) title. This title is won by earning a qualifying score in both the open B and the utility B classes on the same day at the same obedience trial. Do that on nine other days and the title is yours.

Fun Facts

To date no Bulldog has earned an OTCH championship.

Still craving more obedience? There is always the Obedience Trial Championship (OTCH) title, which is awarded to dogs who win a utility class and an open class and then, for good measure, win another one of those classes a second time. A dog must also earn 100 points in competition. Points are awarded on the basis of how many dogs your Bully defeats in the ring, but regardless of how many dogs he defeats, he must finish first, second, third, or fourth in the open and utility classes in to earn points toward the OTCH title.

Informal Obedience Training

What if dog shows had obedience trials that included exercises like "stop chewing that at once" or "don't bark every time the doorbell rings"—practical, everyday stuff like that. After all, how many times will there be ten wallets lying in a pile on the living room floor and we will need our Bully to go over and pick out ours? Why not drag a sofa into a show ring instead, lead a Bulldog in, and as soon as he begins chewing on it, give his owner 15 seconds to get him to stop? The owner who accomplishes that feat in the fewest seconds, wins—and gets to keep the sofa.

Until the AKC wakes up to the need for informal obedience training, Bulldog owners will have to fill in the gaps by spending lots of time with their dogs, socializing and training them properly, and correcting behavior problems before they occur. The following tips will aid in that regard:

- Do not ignore undesirable behavior. It will not go away on its own; do something about it when it happens.
- Distract your Bully when he misbehaves; he has at best a 10-second attention span, so give him a chew bone that tastes better than a chair leg.
- Always reward good behavior, especially when it replaces bad, as in the preceding example.
- In a pinch, resort to those stuffy, formal commands like "*Sit*" and "*Stay*" when the doorbell rings and your Bully begins to race toward the door with every intention of hurling himself against it. What have you to lose except your patience?

Fun Facts

The first American Kennel Club-licensed obedience trial, held in 1936, drew about 200 entries.

So You Want to Show Your Bulldog

Many first-time Bulldog owners could not care less about showing when they bring their puppies home, but after being told several times at the dog park or

BE PREPARED! Choosing a Trainer for Your Bulldog

You do not have to be smarter than the average bear to train your Bulldog entirely at home, but unless you plan to keep your Bulldog entirely at home, you will want him to obey commands as crisply when there are other dogs and people around as he does in the backyard. Obedience classes provide the company of other people and dogs, and chances are you and your Bully will benefit from and enjoy attending classes conducted by a reputable and competent dog trainer.

Leads to dog trainers can be found through the Yellow Pages, the Internet, veterinarians' offices, humane societies, boarding kennels, or dog groomers, but selecting the first trainer you find is like choosing the first vacation resort or a college without bothering to read the other brochures. In selecting a dog trainer, "reading the brochure" means visiting the trainer's home or training location to ask a few questions and to see how his or her dogs behave.

If you ring the trainer's doorbell and a dog inside begins barking and hurling himself against the door, pretend you are seeking directions to the nearest shopping mall and look for a trainer elsewhere. At the very least you will want to know the following about a prospective trainer for your Bulldog:

- How long has he or she been training?
- Is he or she qualified as an evaluator for the Canine Good Citizen program?
- Does he or she hold current membership in the Association of Pet Dog Trainers, the International Association of Canine Professionals, or another dog training or behavior association?
- Does he or she provide written handouts?
- What correction methods does he or she use?
- Does he or she permit treats as training aids?
- How large are his or her classes?
- Do people and dogs receive some individual attention?
- Are all dogs required to have proof of vaccination before starting a class?

the feed store that they "ought to show that dog," they convince themselves that a dog is a show prospect simply because he has a pedigree. Wrong. Pedigrees do not show dogs make. Indeed, most pedigreed dogs are not *show quality*, even if you define "show quality" as meaning good enough to earn a championship. (If the truth be known, many dogs can earn championships if they live long enough and are taken to enough shows by the right handler.)

If you are suddenly overcome by a desire to show the Bulldog you purchased at a pet price, consult the dog's breeder first. Breeders are not opposed to buyers showing ugly ducklings that have turned into swans, but breeders are less than thrilled when less-than-perfect examples of their breeding programs turn up in the show ring accompanied by an overenthusiastic novice exhibitor. So before you enter your Bully in a show, ask his breeder if you can take your boy around for an evaluation. If you bought your dog from a breeder who lives far away, ask a local breeder to evaluate your dog. An ounce of prevention can be worth a pound of disappointment in the show ring.

Where the Shows Are

The AKC recognizes more than 150 breeds of dogs and sanctions roughly 10,000 competitive events each year. These gatherings include conformation shows, obedience trials, and field trials. Many AKC events are advertised in dog magazines and, occasionally, in newspapers; but the best place to look for such events is on the events page of the AKC web site—*www.akc.org/events/static/*. If you simply want to attend a show, locate one near you and you are on your way.

If you are interested in entering your Bulldog in a show, you will need the names and addresses of the superintendents who manage shows. These are the people from whom you can obtain premium lists for the shows you want to enter. A list of superintendents is printed each month in *Dog World* magazine, in the *Events Calendar*, published by the AKC, and in the "Resources" section (see page 179) of this book.

The Premium List and Entry Form

A premium list contains information about a scheduled show and the entry form you need to enter a dog in that show. Premium lists provide the date and location of the show, the names of the judges for each breed eligible to compete in the show, directions to the show site, information about overnight camping facilities, the date on which entry forms are due at the superintendent's office, and lists of special prizes offered at the show.

Breed Truths

Registration papers mean only that a dog is eligible to be registered, not that he is good enough to be shown. Any AKC-registered dog can be entered in a show, but there is a huge difference between a dog that can be shown and a show dog. Anyone can enter a talent contest, but not every contestant has talent.

Premium lists are available from show superintendents. To obtain premium lists for shows in your area, write to one or two superintendents and ask to be put on their mailing lists. If there is a specific show for which you want to obtain a premium list, include that request in your letter or e-mail.

Once an entry form is completed, mail it to the show superintendent with the appropriate fee; fax it, along with a credit card number; or use a convenient online entry form if the show superintendent provides one. Entries cost on average between $25 and $30, and they are usually due at the superintendent's office about two weeks before the day of a show.

Roughly one week before the show, you will receive a confirmation packet from the superintendent. It will contain an entry card, a judging schedule, the number of entries for each breed, and the numbers of the rings in which the various breeds will be judged.

The entry confirmation also contains a facsimile of your Bully's listing in the show catalog. Check this listing carefully to make sure all names are spelled correctly, your dog's registration number is accurate, and your dog has been entered in the correct class. If you find any errors, report them to the superintendent as soon as you reach the show site. You may have to ask two or three people where the superintendent is, but he or she will not be difficult to find.

Types of Shows

You have three types of events from which to choose: the match show, the all-breed show, and the specialty show. The latter two shows (all-breed and specialty) are also known as point shows because dogs competing in them may win points toward championship or obedience titles.

Match Shows Match shows offer inexperienced exhibitors and/or their dogs a chance to learn their way around the ring in a relaxed setting. Although match shows are similar to point shows, no points toward championships or other titles are awarded, nor do match-show judges have to be licensed by the AKC. What is more, puppies as young as three months of age may be entered in a match show. (At point shows puppies must be at least six months old in order to compete.)

All-Breed Shows These are AKC-licensed shows at which all 150-plus breeds recognized for championship competition are eligible to compete for points toward their championship or obedience titles. Entries at all-breed shows regularly exceed 1,000, and shows with 2,000 or even more are not uncommon.

Specialty Shows These are AKC-licensed shows in which only one breed is eligible to compete for championship points and other awards. The Bulldog Dog Club of America holds a national specialty show each year. In addition, regional Bulldog clubs hold their own specialty shows throughout the year.

Group Shows The AKC assigns each of the 150-plus breeds it recognizes to one of seven groups. Bulldogs belong to the Non-sporting group. Occasionally a specialty show will be held with entries limited to dogs of a certain group. This kind of show is known as a group show.

Which Class to Enter

In conformation shows males (which are called *dogs*) and females (which are called *bitches*) are competing for points that will make them champions. They are also competing for best-of-breed, best-in-group, and best-in-show awards.

A dog or a bitch must earn 15 points to become a champion. Those points can be earned one, two, three, four, or five at a time, depending on the number of other entries a dog or a bitch defeats in competition. Before explaining what distinguishes a one- from a two- from a five-point win, we should describe the kinds of classes offered at all-breed and specialty shows.

All dogs and bitches that have not earned their championships compete against other nonchampion members of their breed and sex for points toward the championship title. Nonchampion dogs or bitches, known as class dogs or class bitches respectively, may be entered in any of the first seven classes described in the table on page 125. Limitations of time and space preclude a discussion of the reasons for entering your dog in these classes. The breeder from whom you acquired the dog should be able to offer you guidance in that regard.

The Mechanics of Judging

Nonchampion (or class) dogs usually are judged before nonchampion (or class) bitches. In each class the judge awards first- through fourth-place ribbons if the size and quality of the class warrant them. After all classes have been judged, winning dogs from the various classes return to the ring immediately for the winners class. The winner of that class—i.e., the winners dog—receives points toward the champion title.

Breed Truths

Winners in the different classes offered at conformation shows are nominally selected because they most closely approximate the kind of dog described in the written standard for the breed. In reality, breed standards are constructed broadly enough to allow men and women of goodwill to interpret them differently. As a result, a dog that was best in show on Friday might not even be best in its breed at the following day's show. Indeed, one dog show judge has written that the continuing success of the dog fancy is based to an extent on inconsistent judging. Otherwise, the same dogs would win all the time and few people would bother to enter their dogs in shows.

Class bitches are judged in the same class sequence as class dogs. Immediately after winners bitch has been chosen, the best-of-breed class is held. This class is for champions (also known as specials) of both sexes and for the winners dog and the winners bitch at that day's show. In the best-of-breed class, all dogs and bitches compete for best of breed and best of opposite sex. In addition, the winners dog and the winners bitch compete for the best-of-winners ribbon.

At specialty shows the competition is over at this point. In all-breed shows best-of-breed winners return later in the day to compete in their respective groups. The best-of-breed Bulldog competes in the Non-sporting group.

Judges award first- through fourth-place ribbons in group competition. Finally, the seven group winners compete for best in show at the end of the day.

Counting Up the Points

The number of points earned by the winners dog and the winners bitch are determined by the number of other class entries those winners defeat. This number, which is based upon the cumulative entries in a breed during the

FYI: Conformation Show Classes

Puppy	For entries between six and twelve months of age that are not yet champions.
Twelve to 18 Months	For entries twelve to eighteen months of age that are not yet champions.
Novice	For entries six months of age and over that have not, before the date of closing of entries, won three first prizes in the novice class, a first prize in bred-by-exhibitor, American-bred, or open classes, or one or more points toward their championship.
Amateur Owner-Handler	For entries at least six months of age that are not champions; dogs must be handled by their registered owners, who may not ever have been professional dog handlers, AKC-approved conformation judges, or assistants to professional handlers (effective January 1, 2009).
Bred by Exhibitor	For entries above the age of six months that are being shown by people who bred and currently own them.
American Bred	For entries above six months of age that were born in the United States from a mating that took place in the United States.
Open	For entries more than six months of age.
Winners	For the winners of any of the classes described above; this class is held immediately after the preceding classes have been judged; but you cannot enter this class in advance, you must win your way into it the day of the show.

preceding show season, may vary from one region of the country to another, from one year to another, and from one breed to the next. For example, during the 2008 show season in Division 2 of the AKC, a division that comprises Delaware, New Jersey, and Pennsylvania, two class (or nonchampion) Bulldog dogs present and competing constituted a one-point show. Seven class dogs present and competing constituted a two-point show. Twelve dogs constituted a three-point show; 19 dogs a four-point show; and 33 or more a five-point show. In bitches, two entries were required for a one-point show; 9 for a two-point show; 15 for a three-point show; 23 for a four-point show; and 38 or more for a five-point show. No dog or bitch can earn more than five points at a time toward championship, no matter how many entries are defeated.

All 15 points needed to become a conformation champion may not be accumulated one or two at a time, however. Two wins must be major wins, that is, wins that are worth three, four, or five points. And those major wins must come from two different judges.

Mathematically, the fastest a dog or a bitch can finish a championship is in three shows. In actuality it takes more shows than that—a lot more for the majority of champions. If you figure that it will take a Bulldog an average of 15 to 20 shows to earn its championship, chances are you will be right more often than not.

Ring Procedure

Upon entering the ring, exhibitors line up their dogs or bitches down one side of the ring or, if the class is large, down two or more sides. Exhibitors then stack their dogs (see "Stacking" page 128) while the judge walks down the line taking a first-impression look at each entry in the class.

The judge then asks the exhibitors to walk their dogs around the ring in a circle en masse. After the exhibitors come to a halt, the judge inspects each entry closely. After the judge has examined an entry, he or she asks the exhibitor to gait (or walk) the dog in one or two patterns (see "Gaiting Patterns" below). Finally, after the judge has inspected every entry in a class, he or she may ask a few individuals to gait their entries again. At that point the judge may shuffle the order in which dogs are standing in the ring before asking the entire class to circle the ring again. The judge will then point to the first-, second-, third-, and fourth-place finishers in the class. These dogs and their exhibitors line up to receive their ribbons while the rest of the class leaves the ring. (In best-of-breed classes, the judge will indicate a maximum of three winners: best of breed, best of opposite sex, and best of winners.)

Practicing at Home

For practical reasons you should teach your Bulldog to walk on a leash (see pages 106 and 130), but you will need to refine that talent for the show ring. In the ring your Bully should be willing to walk smartly at your left side, neither lagging behind nor surging ahead.

Gaiting Patterns Exhibitors usually are asked to gait their dogs or bitches in one or more of three patterns: the circle, the down-and-back, and the triangle. To practice these patterns at home, all you need are your dog, a leash, a 40-by-50-foot (12.2 to 15.2 m) swatch of yard, and a pocketful of small treats.

The secret of showing—for you and your dog—is having a good time. Always begin each practice session with a minute of two of spirited petting and a few treats. You want your Bully to react gleefully to the sight of a leash because he knows there are treats in store and a chance to be the center of attention.

In the down-and-back pattern, your Bulldog walks on your left for 15 or 20 feet (4.5–6.1 m), smartly makes a right U-turn, then walks back to the starting spot. As you bring your Bully to a halt, hold a treat a few feet in front of his face, slightly above eye level, to get his attention. Bulldogs are supposed to look attentive, but if your dog starts to rise up on his hind legs, say *"No"* or *"Down."* Do not give him the treat until he has all four feet on the ground and is standing still for five or ten seconds.

Because dogs are not supposed to sit in the show ring, do not allow your Bulldog to sit down while you are practicing. If he does, just say *"No"* and snap the leash briefly until he stands up.

In the circle pattern, you keep your Bulldog on your left while walking a circle with an 8- to 10-foot (2.43–3.01 m) radius. At the end of each circle bring your Bulldog to a halt, show him the treat, and after he is standing still five to ten seconds, reward him with praise and the treat.

In the triangle pattern, you walk ten to 20 feet (4.5 to 6.1 meters), turn left, walk another ten to 15 feet (3.01 to 4.5 meters), then return to the starting point on the diagonal. Repeat the exhibitor-shows-treat, dog-poses-handsomely routine at the end of each triangle.

You do not have to practice these patterns more than 10 minutes or so every second or third day. After that, practice only as much as you and your dog need to in order to remain crisp.

In addition to teaching a Bulldog good ring manners, leash training should develop the gaiting speed at which a Bulldog looks most natural. In short, you and your Bulldog should look relaxed in the ring. Practice walking in an easy, yet purposeful manner, keeping one eye on the dog and the other on the judge. Do not allow your Bulldog to sniff the ground or to walk with his head drooping. If he begins sniffing or ducking his head, a short tug on the lead will bring his head to the desired position. Do not jerk the leash strongly. The idea is to get your dog's attention, not to lift him off his feet. The leash is a corrective, not a coercive, device.

Stacking This is the art of positioning a dog so as to accentuate his best qualities and minimize his flaws. With the lead on your Bulldog, position him so that he is standing with his front legs foursquare. If necessary, get down on one or both knees and set your Bully's legs in place. If your Bulldog tends to toe one front leg in or out, turn that leg to the desired position (always turn from the top, not the middle, of the leg) and set that leg in place first. Position the hind legs in the same manner. When your Bulldog is looking camera ready, hold a treat a few feet in front of his face, slightly above nose level, so that he will hold that pose for at least a minute.

Do You Need a Handler?

Showing a Bulldog does not require as much fleetness of foot or deftness of comb as some other breeds. A reasonably coordinated and self-confident person should be able to show his or her own Bully. If you prefer, however, you can hire the services of a professional dog handler. A professional handler knows tricks that a novice could be a long time learning, and a professional is known by more judges than

CHECKLIST

Basic Show Supplies

✔ Flea comb
✔ Brush
✔ Cotton swabs
✔ Cotton balls
✔ Paper towels
✔ Facial tissues
✔ Washcloth
✔ Eye drops
✔ Pen
✔ Can opener
✔ Bottle opener
✔ First-aid kit

✔ Food (canine and human)
✔ Spoon
✔ Biodegradable paper plates
✔ Bottled water (preferably from home)
✔ Water bowl
✔ Magazine(s) or book(s)
✔ Dog-waste scooper
✔ Small plastic baggies
✔ Hair dryer (if an emergency bath or touch-up is necessary)

a novice is. Handlers charge about $75 to show a dog, and if they have to take your dog with them overnight, you will subsidize a portion of their traveling, lodging, and eating expenses, too.

Provisions for a Show

The most important items to pack for a show are the entry card and show confirmation, the leash, some treats, a folding chair, and a spray bottle filled with water. (You will need the latter if your Bulldog gets overheated.)

The incidental items packed for a show are determined by personal comfort. Some exhibitors pack enough provisions for a two-month stay in a biosphere. Others pack more conservatively. The checklist above, therefore, is intended merely as a guide.

Fun Facts

Helen Whitehouse Walker devised the first obedience "test" in Mt. Kisco, New York, in 1933 to show off the intelligence of her Poodles.

The Last Words

Training a Bulldog is not so difficult as herding cats, nor is it so easy as operating a sheepdog by remote control. Somewhere between those extremes lies the promised land, a land that you can reach, we promise, if you keep your wits about you and help your Bulldog to keep his wits about him, too.

Leash Training

1 After your Bulldog is comfortable wearing a collar or a harness, attach a leash to it and let him drag the leash around a short while.

2 Pick up the leash and follow your Bully around wherever he wants to go for a minute or two.

3 Holding a treat in your nonleash hand, begin to coax your Bully to follow you. Stay a few steps ahead of him and—without pulling or jerking on the leash—encourage him to come to you for the treat.

4 Within a day or two your puppy will begin to follow you as you walk. If he sits down or balks, use the treat to entice him again.

The *Sit* Command

1 Get your Bully's attention by kneeling in front of him with a treat in one hand.

2 Give the *sit* command, then push down immediately on his hindquarters with your other hand—or scoop his hind legs under him, folding him into a sitting position. If he tries to get up, exert pressure on his hindquarters until he is sitting correctly.

3 Praise him lavishly when he sits, even though you did most of the work, then give him the treat.

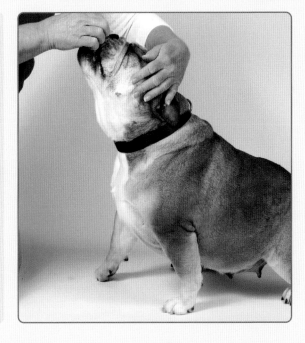

4 Repeat steps one, two, and three several times, then end the lesson. During subsequent practice sessions remain standing when you tell your Bulldog to sit.

The *Stay* Command

1 With your Bulldog on a leash standing in front of you, give him the *sit* command.

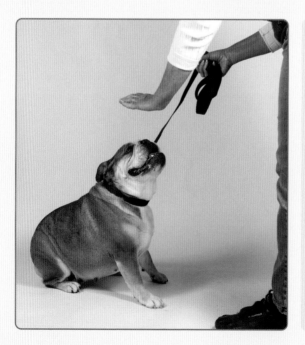

2 After he is sitting, put the palm of your right hand in front of his face as though your were stopping traffic and say "*Stay!*" If he tries to get up, return him to the *sit* position.

3 Gradually increase the length of time your Bully will stay until he can stay for a full minute. Don't test his patience at this point. The attention span of any youngster, canine or human, is relatively short.

4 When your Bully can stay in position for a minute, begin increasing the distance between the two of you. Using a long leash, or a lightweight rope attached to his collar or harness, start with a few steps backward and gradually increase the distance to several yards.

Chapter Eight

Bulldog Grooming

Grooming your Bulldog, like virtue, is its own reward. The more dead hair you remove from your dog, the less you need to remove from the furniture, the rugs, the car, your navel, or your clothing.

Although a Bulldog's coat is short, Bulldogs do shed, and unlike ordinary dog hair, which lies where it lands, Bulldog hair penetrates any available fabric. Once this happens, ordinary vacuum cleaners are powerless against Bulldog hair's tenacious grip. Nothing short of a 95-horsepower, fuel-injected model can begin to deal with entrenched Bulldog hair.

You should be able to keep your Bulldog and your furniture looking well groomed if you brush the former two or three times a week. Ordinarily Bulldogs are not opposed to being groomed if you set about the task with the right treats and the right tools. Before you begin grooming your Bulldog, lay out the implements you will need. Your selection will depend on your purpose—routine maintenance or a red-carpet makeover.

Breed Needs

Brushing your Bulldog not only removes dead hair and skin, but also spreads oil throughout his coat and stimulates the flow of blood.

Grooming Techniques

A well-raised Bulldog puppy should not object to being groomed, but if grooming is a new experience for your Bully, begin to get him used to it as soon as he is comfortable in his new surroundings. Keep grooming sessions short—five minutes or so at first—and space them two to three days apart until your puppy is used to being brushed and groomed.

Choosing a place for grooming your Bulldog is a matter of personality. Type A personalities tend to favor regulation grooming tables from a pet-supply store, and there is much to recommend such devices, including ease of cleanup and a built-in, nonslip surface. On the downside, unless you have

CHECKLIST

Grooming Necessities

- ✔ Brush(es)
- ✔ Flea comb
- ✔ Nail clippers
- ✔ Tick-removal tool
- ✔ Cotton balls
- ✔ Cotton swabs
- ✔ Lukewarm water
- ✔ Mineral oil
- ✔ Toothbrush and toothpaste
- ✔ Petroleum jelly
- ✔ Plastic spray bottle for water
- ✔ Grooming table (optional)
- ✔ Wastebasket or other receptacle for dead hair

Tip: The all-purpose Bulldog grooming tool is a natural-bristle brush or a rubber mitt. Before selecting a brush, test the bristles on your arm. If they cause discomfort on you, they probably will on your Bulldog, too.

If you want to be especially thorough about removing dead hair—or if you have several pounds of hair to remove—use a rubber brush. The only comb you need for a Bulldog is a flea comb.

$800 to spend on a hydraulic grooming table, you are going to have to lift your boy onto the grooming table and off again.

More laid-back personality types just grab a brush and start grooming while they watch television, others toss a rubber mat on top of the clothes dryer or the kitchen table, and some people living in a warm climate use a table on the back patio.

No matter where you choose to do it, grooming a Bulldog does not require a painter's touch, but there are a few techniques to be mastered. Always brush with the lay of the coat. Do not push down constantly on the brush; move it across your dog's body smoothly with your wrist locked.

Helpful Hints

To help prevent the hairs in your Bulldog's coat from breaking when you brush him, spray his coat lightly with water before you begin grooming.

Grooming young puppies and some older dogs may require that you wield the brush with one hand while you steady the dog with the other. If so, place your free hand on the puppy's chest while you brush his back and sides, or place your free hand, palm up, on his underbelly while you brush his hindquarters or neck.

A Bulldog's legs are brushed or combed downward with short strokes. To groom a Bulldog's tail, hold it gently by the tip and brush or comb softly with the lay of the coat.

As you brush your Bully, look for flea dirt, skin rashes, bald spots, and other irregularities in his coat. If you find flea dirt, a flea bath and/or an application of a topical flea fighter is in order. Skin rashes or bald spots suggest a visit to your veterinarian, who can assess the problem and prescribe treatment.

Wiping Out Tear Stains

There is a price to pay for the Bulldog's pretty face, and that price is tear stains, which can be the devil to exorcise once they establish a facehold in a Bulldog. To prevent this from happening, wash your Bully's face with luke-warm water and a washcloth each day—or every other day at least.

If your Bulldog develops tear stains, mix equal parts hydrogen peroxide and white milk of magnesia with enough cornstarch to make a paste. Apply this mixture to the stained areas twice a day, then brush it out with a toothbrush after it has dried into a cake. After the stains begin to fade (you should start to see results in five to seven days), apply the mixture once a day until your Bully's face is showroom new again. Be careful not to get any of this mixture in your dog's eyes.

If hydrogen peroxide, white milk of magnesia, and cornstarch are not your cup of tea, you can use boric acid, boric acid ointment, or a commercial tear-stain remover to remove your Bulldog's tear stains. After you have dried his face, smooth a thin layer of diaper rash ointment over the stained area and dust it with medicated powder. This treatment will cause tears to roll off your Bully's face instead of staining it.

Wrinkle-Free Wrinkles

A Bulldog's facial wrinkles, which contribute to his handsome appearance, may contribute to his discomfort also—and to a dead-fish odor—if they are not cleaned regularly. Wrinkles are like the space between the cushions and the back of the couch. They are a landfill in search of debris. Excess food, tears, or other discharges from the eyes accumulate and, subsequently, fester in a Bulldog's wrinkles, causing them to become red, raw, and infected. A Bully's wrinkles must be kept clean because air cannot circulate through them.

Breed Needs

Do not overlook your Bulldog's nose when grooming him. If it looks dry rather than moist and shiny, dab a little petroleum jelly on it each day until it returns to its normal luster. If your Bully's nose is cracked, apply a coat of Panolog ointment once or twice a day until his nose is repaired.

Two or three times a week—more often if necessary—clean any dirt or caked tears from his wrinkles. A cotton swab that has been dipped in warm water can be used for this task, as can a damp cloth, cotton balls, or baby wipes, including baby wipes with aloe. Instead of warm water, some people dip the cloth or cotton swab into a mixture of warm water and dog shampoo.

Be sure to clean your Bully's wrinkles delicately. Bulldogs are justifiably proud of their faces, and they may take exception to your mucking about roughly in their wrinkles. With patience and bribery, you should be able to overcome any resistance.

After you have mined your Bulldog's wrinkles, rinse them with water if you have used a cleaning agent; dry them thoroughly, then add a layer of petroleum jelly to soothe the skin and to create a water barrier. If you notice bald spots or a rash in your Bulldog's wrinkles when you clean them, take him to the veterinarian to determine whether he (your dog) is growing a fungus.

Brushing Up on Dental Care

Keeping your Bulldog's teeth clean can help to prevent certain diseases of the heart, liver, and kidneys that are thought to be caused by the spread of bacteria from a dog's mouth. Diligent Bulldog owners, therefore, do not allow poor dental hygiene to put the bite on their dogs' health.

Dry dog foods, which ought to make up the bulk of a Bulldog's diet (see page 89), help to a certain extent to reduce plaque—the sticky combination of bacteria, food particles, and saliva that is constantly forming and hardening on a Bulldog's teeth. Unfortunately, the carbohydrates in dry foods stick to the teeth and act as compost for the bacteria that is plaque's main ingredient. (Canned dog foods do nothing to remove plaque. Worse yet, if they contain sugar, that adds to plaque buildup.)

Bulldogs are willing to assist in their own dental care by chewing on rawhide bones, knuckle bones, marrow bones, or bones made of hard nylon. Allow your Bulldog to floss with some kind of bone or specially designed teeth-cleaning toy several times a week.

If plaque is not removed regularly from your Bulldog's teeth—by you or by your Bulldog—it hardens into calculus (tartar) and intrudes between the teeth and gums, creating a tiny sinkhole in which bacteria multiply. These bacteria invade the gingiva (gum), causing it to become inflamed, to swell, and to bleed when probed. This condition, known as gingivitis, is reversible if treated early in its development. If not, it escalates into periodontitis: ulceration of the gums and erosion of the alveolar bone, which holds the teeth in place. Periodontitis is not reversible, and if it is not controlled, the gums and alveolar bone eventually become so eroded that the teeth fall out.

To check for signs of gingivitis, gently but firmly hold your Bulldog's head with one hand and lift his upper lip along one side of his mouth with the other hand. Look closely at his teeth and gums. Repeat this procedure on the opposite side and in the front of his mouth. Then inspect his bottom teeth in the same fashion. If there is

CAUTION

Never use human toothpaste on your Bulldog's teeth. The foaming agent it contains can cause gastric problems in dogs. Avoid using baking soda or salt to clean your dog's teeth. They do not remove plaque effectively, and they contain sodium, which can be harmful to older dogs with heart disease.

a red line along his gums, make an appointment to have your veterinarian check your Bully's teeth.

Other signs of oral disease include morning breath around the clock, avoidance of dry food, resistance to being stroked on the muzzle, brown or yellow crust on tooth surfaces, loss of appetite, and drooling. If your dog exhibits any of these symptoms, call your veterinarian and describe the dog's behavior.

You can assist your Bulldog in keeping his teeth clean by brushing them once or twice a week. Introduce this idea gradually by having a look at your dog's teeth each day. Check them out as you did during the gingivitis inspection, but in addition to just looking, rub a finger along his teeth, first in front of them and then behind them.

When your Bulldog is used to this intrusion into his personal space, substitute a soft-bristle, child's toothbrush or a finger brush made especially for dogs in place of your own finger. You will want to add toothpaste to whatever brush you choose. Your veterinarian will be able to recommend a suitable toothpaste.

The alternative to keeping your Bully's teeth clean is letting your veterinarian do it. He or she will check your Bulldog's teeth at his annual checkup. If the level of tartar buildup or the presence of loose or compromised teeth indicate, your veterinarian will recommend a professional cleaning. This involves anesthetizing your dog, but he will be home that afternoon, ready to sink his shiny, remaining teeth into his dinner.

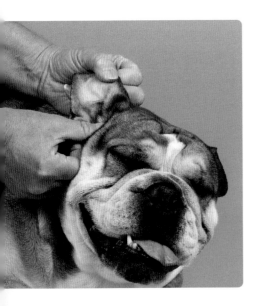

If your Bully is six years old or older, your veterinarian will probably recommend blood tests before cleaning to make sure your Bully is a good candidate for anesthesia.

Ears Looking at You

A Bulldog's ears need to be cleaned regularly because their folded construction discourages air circulation, and infections can grow anyplace where air cannot circulate freely. To keep your Bully's ears clean, all you need are a few cotton swabs or cotton balls and some mineral oil or hydrogen peroxide in a small container.

Dip the cotton swabs or cotton balls into the oil or peroxide and swab the visible parts of the ear carefully. Do not plunge the cotton swab or cotton ball down into the ear canal any farther than the eye can see, or you might do some damage. If you are inspired for some reason to clean your Bulldog's lower ear canal, buy a cleaning solution from your veterinarian and follow the instructions faithfully.

Tell-Tail Signs

Owing to a peculiar rear-end arrangement, some Bulldogs have a small indentation beneath their tails. Not surprisingly this sinkhole is referred to as the tail pocket, another place where the sun does not shine. Some Bullies even have their tails set in this pocket.

Does this not sound like a fun place? Do not laugh: You may be spending more time there than you want if you do not keep your Bully's tail pocket clean and dry. This involves wiping it daily to prevent bacteria from throwing a tailgate party there.

Like a Bully's front-end wrinkles, the tail pocket can be sanitized with a wash cloth, cotton swabs, cotton balls, or baby wipes. Be sure to dry the area in question thoroughly after you have finished cleaning it, and if you just cannot tear yourself away from your work, dab a little antibiotic cream in the pocket for added protection.

If, despite your most diligent efforts, your Bully develops an irritation or an infection in the pocket, see your veterinarian. She or he may prescribe an antifungal ointment, because tail infections are frequently yeast infections.

Trimming Your Bully's Nails

A Bulldog's nails should be trimmed regularly to help prevent him from scratching himself, his playmates, or his two-legged friends while playing. Furthermore, if a Bulldog's nails are too long, he will not stand properly on his toes, and he could suffer a breakdown in the pasterns as a result.

HOME BASICS
Interdigital Cysts

When you groom your Bulldog, inspect the areas between his toes to see if he is hatching an interdigital cyst, which is, in reality, an abscess, not a true cyst. Whatever you want to call it, this swelling is occasioned when pus forms around a foreign body or loose hair that has insinuated itself into the skin between the toes. If your Bully has an interdigital cyst, ask your veterinarian to recommend a treatment that will reduce the inflammation. In addition, make an appointment with your veterinarian to have the hair or foreign object removed if necessary.

Like all dogs that are not used to having their paws handled, a Bully can turn feral when you try to trim his nails. The person from whom you acquired your Bulldog should have begun trimming his nails when he was three weeks old, meaning your Bulldog ought to be tolerant of the process. If he is not so tolerant, you can work on desensitizing him between nail-trimming sessions by holding his paws or stroking them gently for a few seconds when you are petting him or discussing the day's events with him.

Be careful to clip the hooked part of the nail only. Avoid cutting into the quick, the vein inside the nail. Have some styptic powder handy in case you do cut into the quick and it begins to bleed. Dip a cotton swab into the styptic powder and apply it to the bleeding nail. Convey your apologies to your Bulldog—but try to stop short of actual groveling—while the blood coagulates. Be sure to give him a treat afterward.

If clipping your Bully's nails sends you into a swoon, perhaps you should consider a nail grinder, a motor-driven tool with a small, round, abrasive drum at one end that sands away excess nail. For some reason known only to dogs, many of them who try to climb your face when you attempt to trim their nails do not mind the sound or the feel of the grinder once they have gotten accustomed to it. Perhaps they think a grinder cannot cut their quicks. Unfortunately it can. It also can overheat, so be careful when wielding a grinder.

Helpful Hints

Plenty of treats, lavish praise, and a determination greater than your Bulldog's will help to make nail clipping less resemble hand-to-hand combat. Some Bulldog owners recommend putting the dog on a table for this exercise. Others recommend getting someone to hold your Bully while you trim his nails. The idea is to play the game on your court rather than on the floor, where your Bully is apt to think he has home court advantage.

Bath, Rinse, and Beyond

Even the best-groomed Bulldog needs a bath on occasion. When that occasion arrives, your own bathtub is as good a place as any to let the good times flow—unless you have a large, stationary laundry tub in your basement or a portable tub in the backyard.

Before placing your Bully in the tub—before you even go to fetch, lure, or carry him to his bath—make sure the spray attachment, if you plan to use one, is firmly in place, and check to see that you have laid out the implements you will need for the bathing ceremony. Here's a list of what you will need:

- regular or flea shampoo
- brush(es)
- cotton balls
- cotton swabs
- ear-cleaning solution
- several bath towels
- spray attachment for the tub
- mineral oil in a squeeze bottle
- pan or pitcher for rinsing if necessary
- rubber mat
- huge stack of towels
- hair dryer (optional)

Clean your Bulldog's ears if necessary before setting him into the tub. After you have cleaned his ears, put a small wad of cotton into each ear to prevent water from reaching the ear canal and possibly causing infection.

CAUTION

The Bulldog's short, upturned nose may constitute a health hazard in the tub. Because of the short length of his nose, water can easily trickle into it and, from there, into his lungs, causing him to drown. If you are using a spray nozzle, be careful not to get water in your Bully's nose.

Also, when you bathe your Bulldog, never lather past his neck or you risk getting shampoo into his eyes.

Put a few drops of eye ointment into his eyes to protect them from stray shampoo. (If your Bulldog's face needs washing, do that, too, before you bathe him.)

Put a rubber mat on the bottom of the tub to provide secure footing for your Bully. Turn on the water and adjust the temperature, testing it with your wrist. If the water feels too warm to you, chances are your Bulldog will not care for it either. Adjust the water temperature until it is comfortably warm, and do not neglect the house temperature, which should be about 72°F (22°C).

Now that the bathing supplies have been laid out, the bath mat is in place, and the water has been tested, it is time to lift your Bully into the tub. No matter how low the tub is or how much your Bully weighs, do not encourage him to step into or—worse yet—climb into the tub. That way lies injury.

If you are giving your Bully a flea bath, wet his neck thoroughly as soon as you put him into the tub and then apply a ring of flea shampoo to his neck, lathering well. This will help to prevent the fleas on his body from seeking asylum on his face.

Next, wet down the rest of your Bulldog thoroughly, then apply shampoo, working up a generous lather and—if you are using a flea shampoo—

leaving the shampoo in the coat for whatever length of time the manufacturer recommends before rinsing. If you are using a regular shampoo, rinse your Bulldog immediately after lathering.

Do not skimp on water during the rinse cycle. In fact, treat the rinse cycle as a three-step process: Rinse, rinse, and rinse again. At the very least, rinse until the water coming off your Bulldog is as clean as the water going onto him, because traces of soap left to dry on your Bulldog can cause skin irritation and itching. To protect your dog against that outcome, add some vinegar to the final rinse.

After your Bully has been bathed and rinsed, allow him a moment to shake, rattle, and roll while he is still in the tub. Bullies can fling off a surprising amount of water. To keep as much of that water as possible in the tub, close the shower curtain or hold a towel strategically in place while your Bully shimmies and shakes.

Now that your Bully has been shaken and stirred, lift him from the tub and, wrapping him in a towel, begin drying him. As before, do not allow him to get out of the tub on his own.

Use another towel (or towels) to dry him more thoroughly. If the weather is mild, you can allow your Bully to air-dry after you have removed most of the water from his coat. Because baths can have an energizing and, sometimes, a cathartic effect on dogs, take your Bulldog outside for a quick run after toweling him dry.

Should you need to get your Bully's coat as dry as possible as quickly as possible, finish drying him with a hair dryer. If you use your own dryer, use the lowest setting—and test the air on your wrist as you tested Bully's bathwater. A Bulldog's skin is sensitive.

Chapter Nine

The Senior Bulldog

Inside every young Bulldog there is an old Bulldog waiting to get out—like an alien body snatcher in a science-fiction movie. This elderly Bulldog is a patient sort. He does not emerge all at once, but sooner or later he will make his presence known.

All Bulldogs do not age in the same fashion or at the same rate, nor do all the systems in an individual Bulldog age in unison. Therefore, an aging Bully may still hear the sound of kibble clanging into his bowl, but he may not find his way to the kitchen as quickly as he did in the past. Yet no matter how fast or slowly your Bulldog ages, you can mitigate some of the effects of the aging process by providing him with good, proactive veterinary care, an age-appropriate diet, and the extra loving attention his situation requires.

Hear's the Thing

Although a Bulldog's hearing loss may catch you by surprise, it does not happen overnight. Chances are his hearing has declined over many nights and days, but you may not have noticed because your Bully compensated for his hearing loss by relying more on his other senses. He still may bark when you return home, for example, because he picked up your scent, not because he heard the door open.

CHECKLIST

Your Bulldog might be growing old if . . .

- ✔ He mistakes your leg for his favorite tree.
- ✔ He does not hear you calling unless you are looking at him.
- ✔ You can almost hear his bones creaking as he walks.
- ✔ His get-up-and-go seems to have gotten up and went.
- ✔ He sleeps in as though every day is Saturday.

Moreover, you should not assume that your Bulldog's ability to compensate for his diminished hearing guarantees that its cause is age related. Better to have your Bulldog examined by his veterinarian to determine if there is an underlying medical reason—cognitive impairment, for example—that is responsible for your Bulldog's hearing loss.

The Dying of the Light

The loss of vision—because it is most often incremental—does not prevent a Bulldog from keeping his appointed rounds as long as he is in familiar territory. Thus you may not notice your Bulldog's loss of vision unless you rearrange the furniture one day and he takes a tumble when he leaps into the space where the recliner used to be.

Helpful Hints

You can help your Bulldog navigate with confidence by applying common scents to mark specific areas in your house. Use a strong scent like lemon oil or potpourri to mark areas such as stair landings. If your Bulldog has difficulty locating his water bowl, put a drop of vanilla extract on the mat beneath the bowl or, better yet, add a splash of flavored dog water to his bowl when you freshen it each day.

Another scent to which a Bulldog responds favorably is his own. Do not wash his toys unless they begin to glow in the dark. The same applies to his bedding.

FYI: Bulldog Fact

Because a Bulldog's life–expectancy range is eight to ten years, he reaches old age at about his sixth or seventh birthday, a point at which some breeds are just emerging from adolescence.

For the Bulldog with diminishing sight, familiarity breeds comfort not contempt. As long as the food bowl, the water dish, and that comfy, old Barcalounger remain where he expects them to be, even a legally blind Bulldog can get around nicely. He also can manage walks along his favorite routes if you keep him on a lead and give his GPS sufficient time to recalibrate as he sniffs his way along these familiar paths.

Balancing the Scales

As a Bulldog grows older, he is inclined to gain weight even though you are feeding him no more than usual. Two factors are responsible for this phenomenon: his metabolic rate slows down, and his muscles begin to waste.

Breed Truths

Metabolic reduction and muscle wasting conspire to make a six-year-old Bulldog take longer to burn off the calories in a snack than a two-year-old Bulldog.

A Bulldog's metabolic rate is controlled in large measure by the actions of the mitochondria: energy factories in his cells that function like a digestive system, taking in nutrients, breaking them down, and creating energy for the cells. Because the mitochondria become less efficient as they grow older, they do not burn off as many nutrients as they once did, and the body stores those nutrients as fat.

As a Bulldog ages, he is subject also to sarcopenia: muscle wasting. Any decrease in muscle mass is likely to be accompanied by an increase in weight because muscle cells burn more energy than fat cells do.

Sometimes an aging Bulldog's tendency to gain weight can be offset by simply reducing the amount you are feeding him or by feeding him a "lite" or senior dog food: one that contains fewer calories, less protein, less fat, and more fiber than regular food does.

Worrisome Weight Issues

Like many signs of aging in a Bulldog, weight gain may have sinister implications. If weight gain is caused by the accumulation of fluid in the abdominal cavity, a condition known as ascites, heart failure is probably the cause.

CHECKLIST

Signs of Weight Gain

✔ Drooping abdomen
✔ Excess padding about the rib cage
✔ Bulges where the tail meets the body

✔ Exaggerated swing in the walk
✔ Difficulty breathing
✔ Excessive snoring

An elderly Bulldog that begins to look pregnant, and is afflicted by shortness of breath, coughing, or difficult breathing, should be examined by a veterinarian at once.

Cushing's syndrome and Cushing's disease are additional causes of weight gain in elderly Bulldogs. Cushing's syndrome, which occurs when any condition causes the adrenal gland to produce excessive cortisol, is characterized by facial and torso obesity, high blood pressure, stretch marks on the belly, weakness, osteoporosis, and facial hair growth in females. When a pituitary tumor secretes excessive ACTH (adrenocorticotropic hormone), the disorder resulting from this specific form of Cushing's syndrome is referred to as Cushing's disease.

Breed Truths

Bulldogs are as fond of cat food as the next breed is, but cat food is not be suitable for a Bulldog because it is too high in protein.

If a Bulldog exhibits any of the symptoms of Cushing's—and is lethargic, short of breath, and/or less inclined to interact with his owners—he should be examined by a veterinarian at once.

Like weight gain, progressive weight loss in older dogs is cause for concern—perhaps even more so. Weight loss may be an indication of kidney failure, the presence of a tumor, diabetes mellitus, liver disease, or other conditions. If your dog loses weight for two or three consecutive weeks, schedule an appointment with your veterinarian.

Exercise and the Senior Bulldog

Although your Bulldog will slow down as he gets older, he will still need exercise. His activities might be limited by arthritis and muscle atrophy, but you can help him to maintain muscle tone and suppleness, to increase blood circulation, and to improve gastrointestinal motility (the spontaneous movement of the gut) by encouraging him to take part in moderate exercise, the canine equivalent of a leisurely mall walk.

Whatever your aging Bully's idea of sport, do not eliminate the game, just shorten the playing field. If his daily walk consists of three turns around the block, reduce that number to one or two, or replace one extended walk with two or three short walks.

CAUTION

Whenever you go down the stairs into the basement, be sure to close the door so your Bully does not follow you down the stairs head over heels.

Like an aging human athlete, a Bulldog may not know when it is time to retire. Pay close attention to him at the conclusion of a stroll or a round of play. If he seems stressed or if he tires more quickly than he used to, it is probably time to cut back on his minutes. Be especially attentive to labored breathing or the sudden onset of fatigue, as these may be signs of heart disease, and older Bulldogs are more susceptible to heart disease than most other breeds are.

Grooming the Senior Bulldog

Grooming is one aspect of your relationship with your Bulldog that is virtually unaffected by age. If you have been keeping your Bulldog and your furniture looking well groomed by brushing the former two or three times a
week, continue that routine and continue to examine your Bully for external
parasites, skin rashes, bald spots, lumps, and lesions.

The discovery of suspicious lumps or lesions, of course, warrants an
immediate call to your veterinarian. Persistent rashes and spreading bald
spots will need professional attention also.

Some days your Bulldog may not be so receptive to grooming as he usually is. He may fuss and squirm as he did when he was a puppy and was
first becoming acquainted with the comb and brush. Indeed, elderly
Bulldogs can act much like puppies in grooming and in other regards.

Rather than making a federal case out of grooming sessions, make them
shorter and more frequent than usual to accommodate your Bulldog's shortened attention span.

Fighting Teeth and Nails

If you ignore your Bulldog's teeth, tartar accumulates. When it does, gingivitis and weakened tooth structure are sure to follow, making eating a chore at a time when a Bulldog's appetite may be on the decline for other reasons—and making your Bully more prone to secondary infections that could become life threatening.

If you have been remiss in your duties—and if your elderly Bulldog is willing to learn new tricks—review the information about dental care in Chapter 8 and begin brushing his teeth several times a week. If he thinks this idea bites, at least have his teeth cleaned and scaled by your veterinarian at your Bully's semiannual checkups.

Bulldogs are scarcely more happy about having their nails cut than they are about having their teeth cleaned. Granted, an ingrown toenail does not have the same potential for harm as a dose of gingivitis does, but overgrown nails are a source of discomfort nevertheless, and no dog, particularly an aging one, needs another thorn in that crown.

Coping with Hearing Loss

Bulldog owners ought to be as clever as their dogs are about adjusting to their diminished hearing. Avoid startling your Bulldog, especially while he is sleeping or eating. Alert him to your presence by clapping your hands, whistling shrilly if you can, or treading heavily on the floor.

If your Bulldog responds to any or to all of these cues, employ them consistently, and praise him when he responds to them. Praise him also—with the odd treat or an enthusiastic smile—for making eye contact with you, as this will encourage him to look to you for cues more often.

Ironically, dogs who hear less bark more, simply to feel the vibrations in their throats or to "hear" themselves. This barking can be annoying for owners whose dogs have not been given to excess vocalization before.

Caution: Always keep your hearing-challenged Bulldog on a leash when he is away from the safety of his fenced-in yard. He may not hear cars or other dogs approaching, so he depends on you to keep him out of harm's way and to keep harm out of his.

FYI: Skin Conditions in Older Bulldogs

The Bulldog's signature wrinkles about his face, feet, and tail leave him vulnerable to skin problems, and that vulnerability does not decrease with age. Moreover, Bulldogs are frequently allergic to certain foods and to other environmental factors. These allergies can cause skin rashes and irritation that will warrant your attention.

FYI: Symptoms of Disease

Although research does not indicate that elderly Bulldogs are more susceptible to kidney disease, diabetes mellitus, or liver disease than other elderly dogs are, you should be aware of the symptoms of those conditions.

	Kidney Disease	Diabetes Mellitus	Liver Disease
Abnormally colored gums		X	
Appetite changes	X	X	X
Behavioral changes	X		X
Change in activity level	X		
Diarrhea	X		X
Increased thirst or urination	X	X	X
Seizures	X		X
Urinary incontinence	X		
Vomiting	X	X	X
Weakness/exercise intolerance		X	
Weight loss	X	X	X

Personality Changes in the Elderly Bulldog

The older a Bulldog gets, the more conservative he becomes, and a conservative, remember, does not like anything to happen that has not happened before. He is less adaptable to—and less happy about—changes in his environment. Those changes include, but are not limited to, being sent to a boarding kennel, moving to a new house, or welcoming another pet into his family.

You may not be able to refuse the opportunity to head up the new branch of your company halfway across the country, but vacation choices and new pet acquisitions are matters you can control. Put off the trip to Bermuda, and vacation someplace close to home, someplace that welcomes dogs. You will have more fun with your Bully than you will with a bunch of pesky tourists anyway.

Housetraining Revisited

If television commercials can be credited, one out of two Americans past the age of 50 suffers from some form of incontinence. Many elderly Bulldogs will be there and do that, too, but thankfully we will be spared the sight of a Bulldog chanting, "Gotta go, gotta go, gotta go!" like some fool in a commercial.

Nevertheless, your elderly Bulldog may gotta go outside as frequently as he did when he was a puppy—five or six times a day instead of the three or four to which he and you have become accustomed.

If lessened bladder control spills over into incontinence while your Bully is sleeping, the blame may be laid at the feet of weakening muscles. Your veterinarian can prescribe medications to put a clamp on—or at least to dial down—this problem.

Incontinence may spring from something more serious, however, such as a low-grade bladder infection. Dogs are susceptible to bladder infections because the opening to the canine bladder is more lax than it is in humans. As a consequence, bacteria have an easier time gaining access to a dog's bladder and wreaking mischief there.

Bladder infections can be treated with antibiotics, but if that treatment is not effective, your veterinarian may want to run a blood test or take X-rays to check for the presence of a tumor.

Another source of incontinence in older dogs is the onset of kidney failure. As dogs age, blood flow to the kidneys decreases, and the nephrons decrease in number and effectiveness. Consequently, they are less able to regulate the concentration of water as well as soluble substances like sodium salts by filtering the blood, reabsorbing what is needed, and excreting the rest as urine. As a result the kidneys fail to concentrate urine effectively, so older dogs with deteriorating kidney function have to drink and to urinate more often.

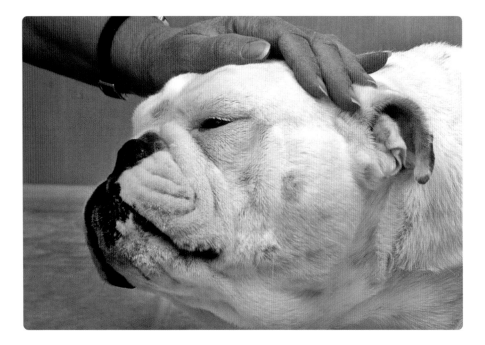

Saying Good-Bye

Time eventually asserts its claim on even the best-loved and most coddled Bulldogs. They become so measured in their movements, so determined in their sleep that they take on the aspect of ghost dogs: their bodies are present, but their spirits are preparing to take their leave.

When your Bulldog reaches this stage, you may have to decide between prolonging and ending his life. That is a decision in which selfishness can play no part.

No matter how much you want to sustain your relationship with your Bulldog, if your veterinarian tells you that your dog is in pain and that the quality of his life is substandard, you owe it to your dog to end that suffering.

The privilege of owning a dog hinges on a crucial bargain: We must add as much to a dog's life as he does to ours. To prolong a suffering dog's

Breed Needs

Because an older Bulldog is more susceptible to disease and less able to defeat it, an annual checkup is no longer sufficient to monitor his health. From the age of six, his annual checkup ought to become semiannual, and it ought to include a chemical blood screen test on each visit. With senior Bulldogs you want the bad news first and you want it early if you hope to give your Bulldog the best chance of warding off or at least controlling a problem.

BE PREPARED! Not an Afterthought

Your efforts to make your senior Bulldog comfortable should include provisions for his care in the event that he outlives you. No doubt you have already made such provisions. Still, you ought to spare a thought for those provisions if you anticipate changes in the circumstances of your Bulldog's prospective guardian.

The brother who always told you that you did not have to worry about your Bully if anything happened to you may have gotten engaged recently. In your relief that he has at last found a woman who will keep him out of the bar scene, did you think to ask how his fiancée feels about dogs—and how she feels about an elderly dog with a creaky bladder who might need Mapquest to find his way in new surroundings?

As long as you are getting personal, have you asked if your future sister-in-law is willing to limit her search for a newlyweds' apartment to those that accept pets?

What about the next door neighbor who was so eager at the thought of caring for a cute Bulldog puppy or a dashing youngster, but who may not be so eager to look after a Bulldog that has reached her Joan Rivers years? Perhaps you need a backup plan.

If you got your Bulldog from a rescue group, you might be able to depend on that group to take him for you. A responsible breeder ought to be of some help in this regard, too.

Because you do not want an elderly Bulldog on four kinds of medications left to the kindness of strangers, having him euthanized if you are going to die before he does may be the final kindness you can do for him—better that than having him spend two or three weeks in a shelter, not get adopted, and then be put to sleep anyway.

If you are fortunate enough to know someone whom you would trust with your Bulldog's life, be sure to provide detailed instructions about his care, feeding, and medication. Providing a small annual stipend to meet those needs is a good idea also.

life because we cannot face saying good-bye is to turn that bargain into exploitation.

If your veterinarian is willing to come to your house to euthanize your Bulldog, arrange for that service so your Bully's final moments will be spent in familiar surroundings. If your veterinarian does not make house calls, he or she may be willing to euthanize your Bully in your car. This can be a comfort for dogs who are upset by the often palpable tension in a veterinarian's office.

If you must take your Bulldog to the veterinarian's office to be euthanized, arrange to wait in the car until the veterinarian can attend to him. Do not simply hand your dog over to an attendant and take a seat in the waiting room. Your Bully was always there when you needed him—and more than a few times when you did not. You owe it to him to be the last person who holds him when he leaves this body for the next one.

10 Questions About Senior Nutrition

When should I begin feeding my Bulldog a senior food? Veterinarians estimate that a dog spends the last third of his life as a senior citizen. By this measure Bulldogs can be considered elderly from their sixth birthday, but instead of celebrating that birthday with a "lite" dog food cake, consult your veterinarian before changing your Bulldog's diet.

Does an older Bulldog need any special kind of food? Unless your veterinarian tells you otherwise, you may be able to maintain your Bulldog's figure by feeding him his regular food in smaller amounts; or you may have to switch to a product that is lower in calories, protein, fat, calcium, and phosphorus—but higher in fiber—than a regular dog food is.

Is it true that senior Bulldogs need less protein? Not in all cases. If a Bully shows signs of decreasing muscle mass—a common by-product of aging—he may need more protein. In addition the theory that aging dogs should be fed less protein to prevent or to minimize kidney disease has not been borne out by nutritional research.

Does a senior Bulldog need supplements? Only if he suffers from some condition that can be alleviated by them. Consult your vet-erinarian before beginning any supplemental regimen. Oversupplementation can be fatal t your Bulldog.

What are some of the con-ditions that can be helped by food supplements? Arthritis is one. If your Bully is arthritic, your veterinarian may recommend a daily supple-ment containing glucosamine and chondroiti to help keep your Bulldog's arthritic joints healthy. Your Bulldog also may benefit from supplement if he is no longer able to absorb sufficient quantities of vitamins, minerals, an electrolytes through his intestinal tract, or if he loses too much of these critical substance through his kidneys and urinary tract.

What should I do if my Bulldog suddenly refuses to eat? If this symptom persists for two consecutive meals, consult your veterinarian, who will more than likely recommend blood work to make sure your Bully's loss of appetite is not the result of some disease.

What do I do if my Bulldog appears to be healthy but he still refuses to eat? If he normally eats dry food the size of golf balls, moisten it with warm water—if you do not d so already—to make it easier for him to chew Otherwise, switch to a smaller kibble.

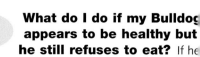

8 **Is it safe to warm my Bulldog's food in the microwave?** Yes, as long as you remember to take the spoon out of his bowl first. Warming moistened dry food—or wet food if that is what you feed—in the microwave helps to increase the food's natural aroma. Ten seconds or so at half power should be sufficient. Do not forget to stir the food and to test it with your finger before giving it to your Bulldog lest he flash-fry his tongue on a hot pocket.

9 **What else can I do to perk up my dog's appetite?** If you have been feeding only dry food, add a few tablespoons of wet food to his bowl, or switch to wet food entirely. You also could spice up his bowl with a small amount of cooked chicken and broth or a cooked or boiled egg. With your veterinarian's approval you could add bacon drippings, hamburger grease, or baby food to your dog's meals.

10 **How many times a day should I feed my elderly Bulldog?** Generally, you should feed him as many times a day as you were feeding him when he was in his prime—i.e., one or two meals a day. If your Bulldog appears to lose interest in his food, perhaps you can make it seem more attractive by feeding him less of it more often—say, three times a day—an approach that mimics the small-plates trend in human restaurants.

Chapter Ten

Special Considerations

W e have saved the worst for last in this book. The "worst" being described by terms such as *keratoconjunctivitis sicca*, *luxating patella*, *femoral head excision*, *hypoplastic trachea*, and other genetic maladies to which a Bulldog is vulnerable. Fortunately, not every Bulldog suffers from these maladies, but their incidence is such that they merit this chapter and the sober consideration of potential Bulldog owners.

Dog breeders often talk about "improving the breed," but Bulldogs never have a say in these conversations. If anyone were to ask Bulldogs how they might want to be improved, they might reply that they would like to do their own breeding, for starters, something few Bulldogs get to enjoy without human intervention. Bullies also might like to be able to go for a good walk on a warm day without risking heat prostration. They might like to be able to deliver their young without the imposition of a C-section. They might further wish that they were not prone to cherry eye, breathing difficulties, sleep apnea, crippling skeletal defects, and a host of skin disorders—not to mention that gas problem.

CAUTION

The chances of your Bulldog's breathing normally vary with his weight: the fatter he is, the more difficulty he will have breathing.

Breathing Difficulties in Brachycephalic Breeds

Brachycephalic (short-face) dogs such as the Bulldog, Boston Terrier, Pekingese, French Bulldog, Lhasa Apso, and Shih Tzu are prone to breathing difficulties. These dogs have been bred with purpose and forethought to have short muzzles and noses, but along with these attributes come breathing passages that are too often undersized and/or flattened. Therefore, brachycephalic dogs are subject to varying degrees of obstruction to their airways (windpipes).

Brachycephalic Airway Obstruction Syndrome

The physical abnormalities underlying Brachycephalic Airway Obstruction Syndrome (BAOS) are an elongated and fleshy soft palate and narrowed, pinched nostrils. Many Bulldogs also display smaller-than-average tracheas (windpipes) and everted laryngeal saccules (a condition in which tissue just in front of the vocal cords is pulled into the trachea, partially obstructing airflow). The results of BAOS range from noisy breathing to collapse.

Breed Truths

Although BAOS (brachycephalic airway obstruction syndrome) is so common as to be accepted as normal for brachycephalic breeds, it causes serious physical problems and discomfort for individuals within those breeds. Therefore, Bulldogs with pronounced breathing difficulties—especially those that have required surgery to correct airway obstruction—should never be used for breeding.

The seeds for BAOS are planted in the Bulldog standard (see Chapter 1, page 11), which mandates that a Bully's face should be dramatically short, as should the distance between the tip of his nose and its placement deep between his eyes. You do not have to be a structural engineer to figure that this arrangement puts the squeeze on the apparatus involved in normal breathing, nor do you have to be a betting person to wager that Bulldogs are more prone to developing BAOS than any other breed.

Although most brachycephalic dogs snuffle and snore to some degree, they may exhibit no additional consequences. Many, however, will be plagued by breathing difficulties, coughing, gagging, sleep apnea, a decreased tolerance for exercise, and the occasional fainting episode. BAOS also puts an increased strain on the heart.

BAOS further dictates that overheating is especially dangerous in affected breeds because increased panting (the normal mechanism by which dogs cool themselves) can cause further swelling and narrowing of the airways, which are already constricted. This, in turn, increases your Bully's anxiety, which, in turn, causes him to pant and so on.

The good news does not stop here. BAOS can lead to gastrointestinal problems because dogs working hard to breathe have trouble coordinating breathing and swallowing. This can result in vomiting, gagging, or aspiration pneumonia if an unfortunate dog aspirates (breathes in) saliva or food particles. Finally, brachycephalic dogs are at an increased risk for difficulties if they have to be anesthetized.

Short-term relief of airway obstruction can be obtained through oxygen therapy and corticosteroids, but severe anatomical faults that compromise breathing must be corrected through surgery. Typically this involves widening the air passages at the nostrils and removing some of the fleshy soft palate.

Elongated Soft Palate

The soft palate—an extension of the hard palate, which forms the roof of the mouth—functions as a mobile flap that prevents food and water from coming out a Bulldog's nose when he swallows. An elongated soft palate hangs in front of a Bully's airway or falls into his throat when he inhales.

Soft palates do not always appear elongated early in a Bulldog's life, but the palate grows while a Bulldog's head does not. Therefore, he develops an "elongated" soft palate. Symptoms of this development include noisy breathing during periods of excitement, spirited exercise, or agitation. A Bulldog with an elongated soft palate may gag frequently from attempting to clear his airway. Also, he may spit up foam and saliva when he eats or drinks. In dire straits, his tongue may turn blue. These symptoms, particularly the blue tongue, are your cue to phone the veterinarian.

Breed Truths

Elongated soft palate is a relative and somewhat misleading term. Actually, the elongated palate is "normal" in length but too long for the radically short Bulldog head.

The diagnosis of elongated soft palate can be made only while a Bulldog is anesthetized. Brachycephalic breeds such as the Bulldog generally have thick tongues, which make a visual inspection of the larynx difficult, not to mention self-defeating, while a patient is awake. Yanking on a dog's tongue to get a look into his throat becomes counterproductive if his tongue turns blue when the dog is stressed.

When a Bulldog is anesthetized, an elongated soft palate extends past the tip of the epiglottis (the entrance to the airway) by several millimeters (0.16 inch). In severe cases the soft palate intrudes into the opening of the larynx.

FYI: Sleep Apnea

Humans and Bulldogs have one trait in common that they share with no other animals: obstructive sleep apnea, a blockage in the airway that dams up the air coming into the throat. Without a sufficient flow of air, respiration stops during sleep apnea. The gap in breathing can last from a few to several seconds and can occur multiple times a minute. After one of these episodes the Bully or human will start breathing normally—or snoring normally—again.

Because Bulldogs that suffer from sleep apnea also suffer from other breathing disorders, the measures taken to manage their effects also help to lessen or eliminate episodes of sleep apnea.

If soft palate reduction surgery, or "resectioning," is needed, it is best done after a dog is roughly a year old and the palate has stopped growing. This procedure can be accomplished with a scalpel blade or scissors, but a CO_2 laser is the preferred technique because it cauterizes the "excess" tissue as it is removed, thus reducing bleeding, swelling, and recovery time. For two or three weeks following soft palate surgery a Bulldog should eat soft food only because kibble is too painful to swallow and too irritating to the throat.

Hypoplastic Trachea

This condition is caused by an abnormal growth of the rings of cartilage in the trachea. The more the cartilage grows, the narrower the airway becomes and the more trouble a dog has breathing.

Hypoplastic trachea occurs most frequently in young brachycephalic dogs, and among the members of that class, it occurs most frequently in Bulldogs, who have comparatively small tracheas. It seldom occurs in a vacuum, but often is present in the company of elongated soft palate and other components of BAOS.

A congenital condition—i.e., one present at birth—hypoplastic trachea causes shortness of breath, wheezing, the occasional gooselike honk, and, in extreme cases, collapse, particularly after vigorous exercise or excitement. These problems begin when a Bulldog is about five or six months old.

Hypoplastic trachea can be diagnosed by an X-ray. Mild cases can be managed by limiting a dog's weight and by moderating his exercise. If this approach does not succeed, treatment with theophylline, which belongs to the class of medications known as bronchodilators, may be necessary.

Tracheal Collapse

If the rings of the trachea become weak, they may no longer support the soft material between them, material that lines the trachea. When this happens, the trachea is partially obstructed by that material, and a Bully has difficulty breathing.

Tracheal collapse can be diagnosed with X-rays. Whenever possible a positive diagnosis should be confirmed by tracheoscopy, direct examination of the trachea with an endoscope or bronchoscope. Bulldogs with tracheal collapse should not be subjected to irritants such as cigarette smoke or excessively dry or dusty environments. Do not use a choke collar on a Bulldog with a collapsed trachea, and if he is the kind who strains at the leash when you walk him, switch to a harness.

Long-term maintenance of a Bulldog with a collapsed trachea begins with getting any coughing under control to prevent inflammation of the tracheal membranes. There are several medical paths to that destination, and your veterinarian can suggest one for you.

If cough suppression does not control inflammation in a Bulldog with a collapsed trachea, low doses of prednisone or another corticosteroid should be used. Antibiotics also may be necessary if there is any reason to suspect that a secondary bacterial infection might be present. If a collapsed trachea fails to respond to medical therapy—or stops responding to it—surgery becomes an option.

Stenotic Nares

Most Bulldogs are born with stenotic nares (pinched nostrils), a condition in which the opening of the nostril is more narrow than the average dog's, and the cartilage separating the nostrils is softer. When a Bulldog with pinched nostrils breathes, the cartilage closes in, further limiting his breathing capacity.

Stenotic nares can be diagnosed simply by looking at the size of the openings into the nostrils. If necessary, your veterinarian can remove a small piece of the wall of each nostril so that your Bully can breathe more freely.

Stenotic nares are caused by congenital malformation of the nasal cartilages brought about by selectively breeding dogs with short noses. Although stenotic nares are present at birth, clinical signs of respiratory difficulty often do not begin until a Bully is several years old.

A Hitch in the Giddyup

Breathing difficulties are not the only problems that beset Bulldogs. The breed is also prone, excessively so, to hip dysplasia (a malformation of the hip joint) and, to a lesser extent, to luxating patella (the canine equivalent of a trick knee).

Breed Truths

The majority of Bulldogs, no matter where they were bred, suffer from hip dysplasia. Champion bloodlines do not guarantee that a Bully will be free of genetic disorders.

Hip Dysplasia

In dogs affected by hip dysplasia, the head of the femur (thighbone) does not fit properly into the acetabulum (hip socket). Eventually the hip joint

FYI: Hip Dysplasia Surgery

Hip dysplasia can be treated by one of the following surgical procedures:

Pectineus tenotomy, a largely obsolete procedure, involves cutting a section of the pectineus tendon and/or muscle. Veterinarians do not know precisely how this surgery relieves pain, but it helps in some cases. It does not help to prevent the onset of arthritis or reduce its severity. Moreover, the relief provided by pectineus tenotomy is temporary in some cases.

Femoral head excisions, as their name denotes, are procedures in which the femoral head (ball portion) of the hip is removed. Because arthritis develops as the femoral head rubs abnormally in the hip socket, removing the femoral head—and thus the bone-to-bone contact—relieves the pain. After the femoral head has been removed, a piece of muscle or joint tissue is placed between the femora and the hip socket. Scar tissue that forms as a result serves to support the leg.

Dogs weighing 45 pounds (20.25 kg) or fewer are candidates for femoral head excisions because they regain most of their mobility after surgery. Bigger dogs do not respond as well to this surgery because the scar tissue cannot support heavier weight.

The recovery period for femoral head excisions can be four to six months. It also can be uncomfortable, but because there are no exercise restrictions, patients recover more quickly the more exercise they get.

Triple osteotomy of the pelvis (TOP), a relatively new procedure, does not prevent hip dysplasia but can prevent the arthritic pain that accompanies it. To qualify for TOP, a Bully must be at least seven months old and show signs of partial dislocation of the hip. The femoral head and the acetabulum must be normal in shape, and there must be no arthritis present. Finally, TOP surgery must be performed as soon as possible after a diagnosis has been made in order to prevent arthritis.

In TOP surgery the femora is set into the acetabulum after cutting the femora in three places and rotating the acetabulum so that the femoral head rests in it securely. The femora, after it has been cut, is held in place with a stainless steel plate and screws—or by a combination of screws and wire—which become a permanent part of a Bully's anatomy.

TOP is the most involved and difficult of the surgeries. Its recovery period ranges from six to nine weeks, during which a patient is not allowed to use stairs, walk on slippery floors, or go outside unless on a leash.

Total hip replacement (THR) is a procedure in which the femoral head is replaced with stainless steel and the hip socket with high-density plastic, using an artificial hip made for dogs. This surgery can be performed at any age after skeletal maturity occurs. Underlying illnesses or skin infections must be treated before surgery.

In THR the femoral head is cut off at a determined angle, and then all tissue is removed from the marrow cavity of the thighbone. A trial prosthesis is inserted into the thighbone to ensure a proper fit.

Cartilage and some underlying bone are then removed from the hip socket, and the plastic hip socket is cemented in place. The marrow cavity of the thighbone is filled with cement, and the prosthetic femoral head inserted. After the cement has hardened, the prosthetic ball is locked into the socket and the surgical site is closed.

THR patients are discharged two days after surgery. They are subject to the same restrictions as dogs who undergo TOP. Six weeks after surgery a dog is allowed full mobility.

FYI: Luxating Patella Severity Chart

Grade I	The patella slips out of position and, in time, slips back into position without having to be manipulated. A dog may learn to coax his patella into place by shaking his leg vigorously.
Grade II	The luxated patella does not return to its normal position without manipulation.
Grade III	The patella is permanently luxated; it can be manipulated into position but will not remain there long.
Grade IV	The luxated patella cannot be manipulated into place, period.

becomes unstable, causing inflammation and weakness. In severe cases of hip dysplasia, painful and sometimes crippling arthritis is a Bulldog's fate.

Although hip dysplasia is hereditary, a Bulldog whose genetic makeup will lead to its development is born with apparently normal hips, and his condition cannot be diagnosed with any certainty until he is six to ten months old. By then pain is a fact of life for that dog.

His owner(s), however, may not be aware that anything is wrong. Bulldogs are tough, and even though a Bully has been afflicted with hip dysplasia since he was two to four months old, he has learned to live with the pain. He may favor his sore leg occasionally, or he may be less active than usual. Otherwise he will not let on that anything is wrong.

Hip dysplasia can be alleviated through surgery, which has been reported to provide striking improvement in a dog's personality and activity level. Older dogs with mild cases of hip dysplasia can be treated with pain-reducing medication.

Luxating Patella

This condition occurs when the patella—the small, flat, moveable bone at the front of the knee—slips out of place, "place" being the center of the dog's knee joint, within the patella ridges. Luxating patella, which affects the hind legs only, is classified into four grades (see chart above).

A Bulldog with luxating patella favors his affected leg when he walks, and when he runs, he lifts it, setting it down every few steps. Occasionally a dog with Grade I luxating patella who is running at warp speed may appear to run normally, but as soon as he stops running, he probably will begin to favor his "bad leg" again.

Luxating patella occurs in dogs of all ages. With the exception of a small percentage of dogs that sustain a patellar injury, the condition is inherited, excess weight being an aggravating factor, not a cause. Luxating patella can be corrected by surgery. It can be prevented by not using affected dogs for breeding.

The Eyes Frequently Have It

The Bulldog is the potential heir to several eye problems. These include keratoconjunctivitis sicca, cherry eye, pigmentary keratitis, and entropion.

Keratoconjunctivitis Sicca

Keratoconjunctivitis sicca, commonly known as "dry eye," is an inflammation of the tissue that covers the interior surface of the eye and the lining of the eyelids. The immediate cause of keratoconjunctivitis sicca (KCS) is insufficient tear production, but the remote cause rarely can be determined.

Roughly 10 percent of KCS cases can be charged to drug toxicities, viral infections, facial nerve trauma, and congenital defects that result in a dog being born with malformed tear glands. Evidence suggests the remainder of KCS cases are related to an immune system deficiency that fools an animal into mistaking parts of its body for foreign invaders and then setting out to destroy those invaders. According to this theory, a Bulldog's immune system may destroy the glands responsible for tear production, rendering him unable to produce sufficient tears.

Breed Needs

Most dogs with dry eye will need eye drops of one sort or another, several times a day, for the rest of their lives. A lucky few may begin producing sufficient tears again on their own, and drops might no longer be necessary, but do not bet the ranch on it.

This leaves a Bully between a rock and a dry place, because tears are vital in maintaining the health of the cornea. They provide moisture and lubrication; they flush out debris; they supply oxygen and nutrients to the cornea; and they possess antibacterial properties that protect against infection. Without adequate tear production, eye infections are common, because bacterial organisms grow on the eye if the bacteria-fighting agent in tears is not present in sufficient quantity. Moreover, dust and pollen accumulate in the eye if it is not lubricated properly.

If your Bulldog exhibits any of the symptoms of KCS, call your veterinarian. KCS, if left untreated, will lead to corneal ulcers, which may lead to blindness.

CHECKLIST

Symptoms of Keratoconjunctivitis Sicca

✔ Squinting and/or rubbing the eye
✔ Dry, dull, or opaque cornea
✔ Reddening of the eye

✔ Mucus accumulates frequently in the corners of the eye(s)
✔ Eye appears to be stuck shut

Dry eye is not difficult to diagnose. A veterinarian hooks a tiny strip of absorbent material called a Schirmer tear test strip into a corner of the eye. After giving tears a minute or so to migrate up the strip, the veterinarian measures the wet area of the strip and compares it with normal tear-production values. If tear production does not measure up, the diagnosis becomes dry eye.

Treatment of KCS typically consists of applying artificial tears, an over-the-counter medication, several times a day to the affected eye(s). In addition, treatment usually involves antibiotics, corticosteroids, and mucolytic agents that help to break up the mucus accumulations associated with KCS.

Cyclosporine, an immunosuppresive agent produced by the soil fungus *Beauveria nivia*, also relieves the symptoms and discomfort associated with KCS. A commercial eye ointment containing cyclosporine has been effective in treating four out of five patients with dry eye.

Applied twice daily to the affected eye(s), cyclosporine can keep a Bully's immune system in check so that the tear glands are not destroyed. In addition, it may stimulate tear production. Cyclosporine therapy is most effective if it is begun during the early stages of KCS.

Cherry Eye

The Bulldog's third eyelid (nictating membrane) is located at the inside corner of each eye, between the lower eyelid and the eyeball. The third eyelid contains a tear-producing gland that contributes about one-third of a Bulldog's normal tear volume. The third eyelid protects the eye through the containment of tears and their distribution over the surface of the eye.

When the gland in the third eyelid suffers a prolapse—an event that is often accompanied by an enlargement of the gland—a scary-looking mass that resembles steak tartare protrudes from the inner corner of the eye. This development is commonly known as "cherry eye."

Restoring the prolapsed third eyelid gland to its normal position will preserve tear production and do wonders for a Bulldog's appearance. This operation is especially critical for Bulldogs because they also are prone to developing dry eye.

The most frequently used and successful technique for repairing cherry eye is the conjunctival mucosa pocket, a procedure in which a pocket is created to hold the prolapsed gland. The pocket is then closed with fine, absorbable opthalmic sutures. In a similar procedure the gland is secured in its original position with opthalmic sutures but without the creation of a special pocket to hold the gland. In one procedure that is not recommended, the third eyelid gland is removed, often leaving a Bulldog with severely restricted tear flow and, ultimately, a bad case of dry eye.

Cherry eye surgery does require general inhalation anesthesia, but a Bully can go home the day of his surgery. His third and lower eyelids may be swollen and red. That is to be expected, as is frequent washing of the eye with saline solution to keep the eye clean of discharges, which trap bacteria.

A Bully may cough occasionally for several days following any surgery, a reaction to soreness of his airway caused by the insertion of the tracheal tube

during anesthesia. If his coughing becomes severe, call your veterinarian or canine ophthalmologist.

A Bulldog's activities should be restricted during the first two weeks after surgery to enhance retention of the third eyelid gland. If he rubs at the surgically repaired eye, he should be distracted with treats, pets, or a restraint collar.

Pigmentary Keratitis
This condition is characterized by the deposition of pigment or melanin on the surface of the eye by the cornea in response to unrelieved irritation or inflammation. Pigmentary keratitis is nature's way of telling Bulldog breeders they have gone too far in their quest for facial extremity, for as breeders have shortened the Bulldog's muzzle, they also have created the Bulldog's excessive nasal folds and shallow eye sockets. The latter cause the eyes to protrude, and if they protrude too much, the eyelids cannot fully cover and protect the cornea, nor can they distribute tears effectively over the surface of the eye. This condition is known as lagophthalmos, and it is one of the causes of prolapsed eyes and dry eye. Other irritating factors include ingrown eyelashes (trichiasis), aberrant eyelid hairs (distichiasis), and trauma to the eye.

Pigmentary keratitis can be permanent if the cause of the irritation or inflammation is not removed—by surgery if necessary—be it excessive nasal fold tissue, ingrown hairs, or dry eye. After the cause of the problem has been eliminated, superficial deposits of pigment on the eye can be treated with topical eye medications. Pigment deep within the cornea may not be so easily treated, and if it impairs a Bulldog's vision, it should be removed surgically if possible.

Entropion

Entropion is a condition in which all or part of the margin of a Bulldog's eyelid—most commonly one of his lower eyelids—rolls inward. As a result the hair from the eyelid skin rubs on the corneal and conjunctival surfaces.

Breed Truths

The success rate for entropion surgery, roughly 90 to 95 percent, is determined in part by a Bulldog's age and the particulars of his entropion.

Most cases of entropion develop by the time a Bulldog is six months old, but sometimes this condition does not appear until after his first birthday. The genetic basis for entropion has not been determined yet, but no one would be surprised if the genes responsible for the head and facial conformation of Bulldogs were listed among the suspects.

When entropion is mild, there is but slight inversion of the eyelid and minimal contact between it and the surface of the eye. There is even a chance, a slight chance, that an immature Bully with a mild case of entropion *may* improve spontaneously as he grows older. Miracles do happen, but they are seldom the safe way to bet. The consequences of mild entropion may be limited to low-grade discomfort and excessive tearing. "Low grade," of course, is in the eye of the beholder, not the sufferer.

Mild cases of entropion in young Bulldogs may be managed medically or with temporary eyelid-tacking sutures. Surgery might be delayed until the age of four to six months, except in severe and complicated cases.

When entropion is severe, however, pain is chronic, and the cornea becomes critically irritated or damaged from constant abrasion, which wears away the corneal surface and can lead to the formation of deep ulcers in the cornea.

CAUTION

Most Bulldogs with entropion squint. The affected eye is reddened or inflamed, and because a Bulldog is in pain, he may scratch at the eye, possibly doing further damage. Left untreated, severe eye infections may develop.

Entropion can be corrected by surgery in which a small incision is made below the eyelid and a small portion of skin is removed. When the two sides of the incision are sutured, the incision pulls the border of the eyelid downward into a normal position.

Fold Dermatitis

Fold dermatitis is an inflammation of the skin folds that occurs in dogs with—ta-da—loose skin. The same folds that protected a Bulldog during bullbaiting now serve as traps for moisture and bacteria. Fresh air being an infrequent visitor to the depths of a Bulldog's wrinkles, the skin in those dark, forbidding canyons can become red, raw, infected, and putrid smelling.

As they do in other categories, Bulldogs top the leader board of candidates for this condition. They are especially susceptible to fold dermatitis in the face and tail areas, where lip, facial fold, and tail dermatitis set up housekeeping.

Fold dermatitis can be prevented by keeping a Bulldog's skin folds clean and dry. In a perfect world this can be accomplished with twice- or thrice-weekly cleaning, but some Bullies will need to have their folds cleaned virtually every day.

Use a damp cloth, cotton balls, or baby wipes to clean a Bulldog's skin folds. Some Bulldog owners recommend using baby wipes with aloe because it soothes and helps to moisturize the skin.

An effective homemade cleaning agent can be mixed by adding a drop of dog shampoo to a cup of warm water. Use a cotton ball to apply the solution gently to the Bully's skin folds, then rinse the folds thoroughly to prevent further irritation.

After the skin of the folds has been rinsed and patted dry, dab a little petroleum jelly into the folds. Petroleum jelly soothes the skin and provides a moisture barrier. Do not use powders or cornstarch to dry the folds because they can clump and irritate the skin.

Helpful Hints

Caveat Emptor

Because not all breeders are as conscientious as they should be, people acquiring a Bulldog should ask the seller who will be responsible for the veterinary bills if a Bulldog should be victimized by an obviously inherited condition later in life.

If, despite your best, most conscientious efforts, your Bully develops raw or irritated skin folds, consult your veterinarian. She or he can recommend a suitable antiseptic ointment or other agent for treating the affected area.

Resources

National Breed Club
The Bulldog Club of America
www.thebca.org

Bulldog Rescue Organizations
The Bulldog Club of America
   Rescue Network
www.rescuebulldogs.org

Arizona
Bulldog Rescue of Arizona
Phone: (480) 238-8383
E-mail: info@bulldogrescueofarizona.
   com

California
Bulldog Club of Northern
   California Rescue
www.thebcnc.org/noframeshome.html

Florida
Buddies Thru Bullies
(South Florida)
www.buddiesthrubullies.org

The Bulldog Club of Central Florida
   Rescue
*www.freewebs.com/centralflbulldogclub/
   bulldogsforadoption.htm*

Tampa Bay Bulldog Club Rescue
Breed Rescue Contact: Karen Radke
6860 South Treshols Place
Homosassa, FL 34446

Georgia
Bulldog Club of Metropolitan
   Atlanta Rescue
E-mail: bcma0797@yahoo.com

Maryland
Chesapeake Bulldog Club of Greater
   Baltimore Rescue
Breed Rescue Contact: Erin J. Corsair
343 S. Chester Street
Baltimore, MD 21231

New Jersey
Mid-Atlantic Bulldog Rescue
P.O. Box 155
Belmar, NJ 07719
E-mail: mabdrescue@aol.com

New Mexico
Chaparral Bulldog Club Rescue
Phone: (505) 744-4626
E-mail: bulldogrescue.newmexico@
   gmail.com

New York
Long Island Bulldog Rescue
Phone: (631) 689-6245
E-mail: bulldogrescue1@aol.com

Ohio
Bullieangel Rescue
E-mail: bullieangelresq@yahoo.com

Tennessee
Smoky Mountains Bulldog Club
   Rescue
www.discoveret.org/smbc/rescue.htm

Texas
Lone Star Bulldog Club Rescue
www.dfwbulldogrescue.org

Virginia
On The Rebound Bulldog Rescue
  Foundation
P.O. Box 1124
Frederick, MD 21702
Phone: (703) 431-8612
E-mail: ReboundRESQ@aol.com

Washington
Cascade Bulldog Rescue
www.cascadebulldogrescue.org

Canine Registries
American Canine Association
P.O. Box 808
Phoenixville, PA 19460
Phone: (800) 651-8332
Fax: (800) 422-1864
www.acacanines.com

American Kennel Club
Registrations
5580 Centerview Drive
Raleigh, NC 27606-3390
Phone: (919) 233-9767
www.akc.org

Canadian Kennel Club
89 Skyway Avenue
Suite 100
Etobicoke,
Ontario, Canada
M9W6R4
Phone: (416) 675-5511
www.ckc.ca/en/

United Kennel Club
100 East Kilgore Road
Kalamazoo, MI 49001-5598
Phone: (616) 343-9020
www.ukcdogs.com/

Health, Welfare, and Medical Organizations
American Animal Hospital
  Association
12575 W. Bayaud Avenue
Lakewood, CO 80228
(800) 883-6301 (Member Service
  Center)
Phone: (303) 986-2800
Fax: (303) 986-1700
E-mail: info@aahanet.org
www.aahanet.org/

American Kennel Club Canine
  Health Foundation
251 W. Garfield Road
Aurora, OH 44202
Phone: (216) 995-0806
E-mail: akchf@aol.com

American Society for the Prevention
  of Cruelty to Animals
424 East 92nd Street
New York, NY 10128-6804
Phone: (212) 876-7700
www.aspca.org

American Veterinary Medical
  Association
930 North Meacham Road
Schaumberg, IL 60173
Phone: (847) 925-8070
Fax: (847) 925-1329
www.avma.org

Canine Eye Registration Foundation
South Campus Court
Building C
West Lafayette, IN 47907
E-mail: CERF@vmdb.org
www.vmdb.org/cerf.html

Delta Society
289 Perimeter Road E.
Renton, WA 98055
Phone: (800) 869-6898
www.deltasociety.org

Humane Society of the
  United States
2100 L Street, NW
Washington, DC 20037
Phone: (202) 452-1100
www.hsus.org

National Animal Poison Control
  Center
Animal Product Safety Service
1717 South Philo Road, Suite 36
Urbana, IL 61802
Phone: (888) 426-4435
        (900) 680-0000
(Consultation fees apply; call for
  details.)
www.napcc.aspca.org

Orthopedic Foundation for Animals
2300 Nifong Boulevard
Columbia, MO 65201
www.prodogs.com

Lost Pet Registries
AVID
PETtrac
3179 Hamner Avenue
Norco, CA 92860-9972
Phone: (800) 336-2843
E-mail: PETtrac@AvidID.com
www.avidmicrochip.com

Home Again Microchip Service
Phone: (800) LONELY-ONE
www.homeagainpets.com

National Dog Registry
P.O. Box 118
Woodstock, NY 12498-0116
Phone: (800) 637-3647
www.nationaldogregistry.com

Petfinders
368 High Street
Athol, NY 12810
Phone: (800) 223-4747
www.petfinder.com

The American Kennel Club
AKC Companion Recovery
5580 Centerview Drive, Suite 250
Raleigh, NC 27606-3394
Phone: (800) 252-7894
E-mail: found@akc.org
www.akc.org/car.htm

Periodicals, All-breed
DOG&Kennel
Pet Publishing, Inc.
4642 West Market Street #368
Greensboro, NC 27407
Phone: (336) 292-4047
Fax: (336) 292-4272
www.petpublishing.com/dogken/

Dog Fancy
Subscription Division
P.O. Box 53264
Boulder, CO 80323-3264
Phone: (303) 786-7306
www.dogfancy.com

Dog World
29 North Whacker Drive
Chicago, IL 60606
Phone: (312) 726-2802
*www.dogchannel.com/
  dog-magazines/dogworld/*

The American Kennel Club Gazette
51 Madison Avenue
New York, NY 10010
www.akc.org/pubs/gazette/

The Bulldogger
(must be a member of the BCA to
receive this publication)
Editorial Office
P.O. Box 136
4300 Town Road
Salem, WI 53168
www.thebca.org/thebulldogger.html

Dog Show Superintendents

BaRay Event Services, Inc.
Contact: Sheila Raymond
203 S. 4th Avenue
Sequim, WA 98382 (Business)
P.O. Box 4090
Sequim, WA 98382 (Mailing)
Phone: (360) 683-1507
Fax: (360) 683-6654
E-mail: dogshows@barayevents.com
Web site: *www.barayevents.com*

Bob Peters Dog Shows, Ltd.
Contact: Bob Peters
1469 NC 96E
Youngsville, NC 27596
Phone: (919) 426-4491
Fax/Phone: (919) 556-6828
E-mail: bob@bpdsonline.com
Web site: *www.bpdsonline.com*

Foy Trent Dog Shows
Contact: Foy Trent
110 E. Canada
Sturgeon, MO 65284 (Business)
P.O. Box C
Sturgeon, MO 65284 (Mailing)
Phone: (573) 881-2655
Fax: (888) 685-8989
E-mail: mail@foytrentdogshows.com
Web site: *www.foytrentdogshows.com*

Garvin Show Services, L.L.C.
Contact: Jane Garvin
14622 SE Old Barn Lane
Damascus, OR 97089-9267
Phone: (503) 558-1221
Fax: (503) 558-9236
E-mail: jane@garvinshowservices.com
Web site: *www.garvinshowservices.com*

Jack Bradshaw Dog Shows
Contact: Jack Bradshaw
5434 E. Olympic Boulevard
Los Angeles, CA 90022 (Business)
P.O. Box 227303
Los Angeles, CA 90022-0178 (Mailing)
Phone: (323) 727-0136
Fax: (323) 727-2949
E-mail: mail@jbradshaw.com
Web site: *www.jbradshaw.com*

Jack Onofrio Dog Shows, L.L.C.
3401 NE 23rd Street
Oklahoma City, OK 73121 (Business)
P.O. Box 25764
Oklahoma City, OK 73125-0764
    (Mailing)
Phone: (405) 427-8181
Fax: (405) 427-5241
Oregon Office:
P.O. Box 4660
Portland OR 97208-4660
Phone: 503.239.1080
E-mail: mail@jack.onofrio.com
Web site: *www.onofrio.com*

Kevin Rogers Dog Shows
Contact: Kevin B. Rogers
1007 W. Pine Street
Hattiesburg, MS 39401 (Business)
P.O. Box 230
Hattiesburg, MS 39403-0230 (Mailing)
Phone: (601) 583-1110
Fax: (601) 582-9909
E-mail: krdogshows@
    rogersdogshows.com
Web site: *www.rogersdogshows.com*

MB-F, Inc.
620 Industrial Avenue
Greensboro, NC 27406 (Business)
P.O. Box 22107
Greensboro, NC 27420-2107
    (Mailing)
Phone: (336) 379-9352
Fax: (336) 272-0864
California Office: (510) 724-4716
Florida Office: (352) 796-1816
Michigan Office: (248) 588-5000

Oregon Office: (503) 649-8549
E-mail: mbf@infodog.com
Web site: *www.infodog.com*

McNulty Dog Shows, Inc.
Contact: Eileen McNulty
1745 Route 78
Java Center, NY 14082-9629 (Business)
P.O. Box 175
Java Center, NY 14082-0175 (Mailing)
Phone: (585) 457-3371
Fax: (585) 457-9533
E-mail: mail@mcnultydogshows.com
Web site: *www.mcnultydogshows.com*

Nancy Wilson
Contact: Nancy Wilson
8307 E. Camelback Road
Scottsdale, AZ 85251-1715
Phone: (480) 949-5389
E-mail: nancronw@aol.com

Rau Dog Shows, Ltd.
Contact: Kathleen Berkheimer
235 S. 2nd Avenue
West Reading, PA 19611 (Business)
P.O. Box 6898
Reading, PA 19610-0898 (Mailing)
Phone: (610) 376-1880
Fax: (610) 376-4939
E-mail: info@raudogshows.com
Web site: *www.raudogshows.com*

Roy Jones Dog Shows, Inc.
Contact: Kenneth A. Sleeper
1105 W. Auburn Drive
Auburn, IN 46706 (Business)
P.O. Box 828
Auburn, IN 46706-0828 (Mailing)
Phone: (260) 925-0525
Fax: (260) 925-1146
E-mail: rjds@royjonesdogshows.com
Web site: *www.royjonesdogshows.com*

Books

Andree, Marie. *The Bulldog: An Owner's Guide to a Happy Healthy Pet*. New York: Howell Book House, 1998.

Dickerson, Michael. *Bulldog*. Allenhurst, NJ : Kennel Clubs Books, 2004.

Ewing, Susan M. *Bulldogs for Dummies*. Hoboken, NJ: Wiley, 2007.

Gagne, Tammy. *Bulldogs* (Animal Planet Pet Care Library). Neptune City, NJ: TFH Publications, 2007.

Gallagher, John. *Guide to Owning an English Bulldog*. Neptune City, NJ: TFH Publications, 1999.

Maggitti, Phil. *Bulldogs: Complete Pet Owner's Manual*. Hauppauge, NY: Barron's Educational Series, Inc., 1997.

McGibbon, John F. *The Bulldog: Yesterday, Today and Tomorrow*. New York: Howell Book House, 1996.

Morgan, Diane. *The Bulldog* (Terra Nova Series). Neptune City, NJ: TFH Publications, 2005.

Williams, Carol and Henry. *Bulldogs: A New Owner's Guide to Bulldogs*. Neptune City, NJ: TFH Publications, 1998.

Online Resources

BulldogsWorld.com
www.bulldogsworld.com

The Bulldog Information Library
www.bulldoginformation.com/

Index

THE TEAM BEHIND THE *TRAIN YOUR DOG* DVD

Host **Nicole Wilde** is a certified Pet Dog Trainer and internationally recognized author and lecturer. Her books include *So You Want to be a Dog Trainer* and *Help for Your Fearful Dog* (Phantom Publishing). In addition to working with dogs, Nicole has been working with wolves and wolf hybrids for over fifteen years and is considered an expert in the field.

Host **Laura Bourhenne** is a Professional Member of the Association of Pet Dog Trainers, and holds a degree in Exotic Animal Training. She has trained many species of animals including several species of primates, birds of prey, and many more. Laura is striving to enrich the lives of pets by training and educating the people they live with.

Director **Leo Zahn** is an award winning director/cinematographer/editor of television commercials, movies, and documentaries. He has directed and edited more than a dozen instructional DVDs through the Picture Company, a subsidiary of Picture Palace, Inc., based in Los Angeles.